CW00518569

Animal Friends to Sew

Animal Friends to Sew

Simple Handmade Decor,
Toys, and Gifts for Kids

SANAE ISHIDA

Photography by Amy Johnson
Styling by Rachel Grunig

SASQUATCH BOOKS
SEATTLE

Copyright © 2020 by Sanae Ishida

All rights reserved. No portion of this book may be reproduced or
utilized in any form, or by any electronic, mechanical, or other means,
without the prior written permission of the publisher.

Printed in China

SASQUATCH BOOKS with colophon is a registered trademark
of Penguin Random House LLC

24 23 22 21 20   9 8 7 6 5 4 3 2 1

Editor: Hannah Elnan | Production editor: Bridget Sweet
Design: Anna Goldstein | Styling: Rachel Grunig
Photographs: Amy Johnson

Library of Congress Cataloging-in-Publication Data
Names: Ishida, Sanae, author.
Title: Animal friends to sew : simple handmade decor, toys, and gifts for kids / Sanae Ishida.
Description: Seattle : Sasquatch Books, 2020. | Includes bibliographical references and index.
Identifiers: LCCN 2019022801 (print) | LCCN 2019022802 (ebook) | ISBN
    9781632172358 (paperback) | ISBN 9781632172365 (ebook)
Subjects: LCSH: Soft toy making--Patterns. | Stuffed animals (Toys) |
    Sewing.
Classification: LCC TT174.3 .I94 2020 (print) | LCC TT174.3 (ebook) | DDC 745.592--dc23
LC record available at https://lccn.loc.gov/2019022801
LC ebook record available at https://lccn.loc.gov/2019022802

ISBN: 978-1-63217-235-8

Sasquatch Books
1904 Third Avenue, Suite 710
Seattle, WA 98101

SasquatchBooks.com

For the extraordinary
Rachel Ann Billings Grunig

Contents

Project List

Introduction

WHEN I WAS A KID, MY mom sewed me a fluffy little bunny doll that I called *Usagi-chan*. I must have been quite a literal child since *Usagi-chan* means "little bunny" in Japanese! She was white and simply made, with small felt flowers adorning one of her ears. I loved her so very much. I still have the bunny doll to this day, forty-plus years later.

There is so much care and attention and love poured into anything handmade, especially when created for little ones. As someone who grew up surrounded by handmade goods, I can attest that they enriched my memories of childhood, filling it with a sense of magic.

My daughter was born in 2006, and though I'd had a vague fantasy of finally developing my crafty side for years, it wasn't until I held my little girl that I was gripped with a sudden desire to sew and sew and sew. I remembered all the sweet toys and clothes that my own mother had made for me and I wanted to create my own version of that experience for my daughter.

And what could be cuter than a handmade animal? My first sewing project for my fifteen-month-old was a ladybug costume, painstakingly hand-stitched out of cheap red and black felt. I had no idea what I was doing; I made some sketches, googled "ladybug costume" (back then, not much was available online), checked out some craft books from the library, and took a stab at it. After three days of sweat and confusion and mounting concern that I might not finish in time for Halloween, I lifted the puffy, unwieldy thing I was sewing and marveled that it actually looked like ladybug wings. I slipped the makeshift straps I designed onto my daughter's shoulders and lo! She looked like an insect! A super-adorable insect! I was so proud of myself, and she emitted babbles and squeals of approval. We both glowed.

I've come a long way in the last ten or so years since I started sewing, and that same ladybug costume would take me a mere three hours to complete now compared with the three midnight-oil-burning days of yore. That sense of accomplishment and joy I got from struggling through that first project has propelled me to make hundreds of toys and clothes for my little girl. I've learned a thing or two, and I still get excited about coming up with sewing ideas and experimenting to bring them to life.

The projects in this book are divided into three main categories of cute creatures to sew: decor, toys, and wearables. Like the Japanese craft books that inspired me when I first started sewing for my daughter, this book is structured with a lookbook section in the front that showcases the projects, followed by step-by-step illustrated instructions at the back. If you consider yourself a beginner, check out the basic sewing primer and embroidery tips sections. And if you have years of sewing experience under your belt, I hope you will enjoy whipping out some quick projects and that they will inspire you to try out variations of your own.

I designed all the projects in this book guided by that glowing feeling I got from the ladybug costume. The designs I've included here are simple, and I wanted the projects to feel easy to create, but I also believe in taking time to put care and attention and love into every stitch. So don't rush it or sweat it, and please enjoy every step, mistakes and all!

LOOKBOOK

Pillows

Polar Bear, Lion, Koala, Bunny, Sloth

PROJECT INSTRUCTIONS: POLAR BEAR, PAGE 55; LION, PAGE 59;
KOALA, PAGE 62; BUNNY, PAGE 65; SLOTH, PAGE 68

Placemats

Cat, Bear

PROJECT INSTRUCTIONS:
CAT / BEAR, PAGE 70

Wall Pockets

Zebra, Reindeer

PROJECT INSTRUCTIONS:
ZEBRA / REINDEER, PAGE 73

Rope Baskets

Cat, Dog

PROJECT INSTRUCTIONS:
CAT / DOG, PAGE 76

Stackable Blocks

Mouse, Raccoon, Bear, Elephant

PROJECT INSTRUCTIONS:
MOUSE, PAGE 80; RACCOON, PAGE 83;
BEAR, PAGE 86; ELEPHANT, PAGE 89

Teether Rattles
Whale, Dove, Bunny Ears

PROJECT INSTRUCTIONS:

WHALE, PAGE 92; DOVE, PAGE 95;

BUNNY EARS, PAGE 98

Terry Cloth Bath Puppets

Panda, Cat, Penguin, Seal

PROJECT INSTRUCTIONS:
PANDA, PAGE 100; CAT, PAGE 103;
PENGUIN, PAGE 105; SEAL, PAGE 107

Quiet Adventures
Felt Book

PROJECT INSTRUCTIONS: PAGE 109

Beanbags

Turtle, Hedgehog, Armadillo

PROJECT INSTRUCTIONS:
TURTLE, PAGE 113;
HEDGEHOG, PAGE 115;
ARMADILLO, PAGE 117

Fishing Game

PROJECT INSTRUCTIONS: PAGE 119

Beanies with Ears

PROJECT INSTRUCTIONS: PAGE 125

Baby Slippers

Fox, Penguin, Raccoon

PROJECT INSTRUCTIONS:
FOX, PAGE 129; PENGUIN, PAGE 133;
RACCOON, PAGE 136

Hooded Capes

Animal with Ears, Animal with
Horn, Animal with Bony Plates

PROJECT INSTRUCTIONS: ANIMAL WITH EARS, PAGE 141;
ANIMAL WITH HORN, PAGE 145;
ANIMAL WITH BONY PLATES, PAGE 149

Bibs

Monkey, Koala

PROJECT INSTRUCTIONS:
MONKEY, PAGE 156;
KOALA, PAGE 159

Backpacks

Sheep, Fox

PROJECT INSTRUCTIONS:
SHEEP, PAGE 163;
FOX, PAGE 168

MAKING

///

Sewing Basics

TO GET YOU STARTED, HERE ARE a few recommendations for tools and materials to create the projects in this book, along with a quick overview of good-to-know stitching tips and tricks.

SEWING TOOLS

SEWING MACHINE: Although I reference a "serger" in a couple of projects, you really only need a sewing machine with a zigzag stitch.

SEWING MACHINE FEET: Unless you are adding buttons to the Quiet Adventures Felt Book (page 109), all of the projects in this book require only a straight or zigzag stitch, so the standard presser foot is all you need.

SEWING MACHINE NEEDLES: I recommend having two types of needles on hand: all-purpose and knit friendly. Knit-friendly needles are typically labeled "ballpoint," "stretch," or "jersey," and any one of those will do.

HAND-SEWING NEEDLES: There are a bunch of hand-sewing needles available, so you might want to test out a few to find your preference.

PINS: My favorites are cellulose tulip-headed pins by Hiroshima Needles for quilting and pinning fine fabrics. They are sturdy but very thin and are great for knits too. However, any kind of pin is great, and there's a plethora to choose from.

"WONDER" CLIPS: These are more of a nice-to-have. With certain fabrics, like faux leather, pins leave permanent holes. These clips serve as an alternative to hold pieces together while you sew.

PINCUSHION/MAGNETIC PIN HOLDER: To avoid an avalanche of loose pins, it's a good idea to keep them contained in an easily accessible way. The classic pincushion is a good choice, but my go-to is a magnetic pin holder that enables me to toss the pin in the general direction of the holder, which keeps my sewing momentum going.

THREAD: The all-purpose polyester variety works great for all the projects.

SMALL SCISSORS: This is handy for snipping all the threads as you sew and easier to use than a regular pair of scissors when clipping curves and corners of seam allowances.

POINT TURNER: There are a number of specially designed point turners available, but a chopstick or the wrong end of a small paintbrush will do just fine too.

BODKIN/SAFETY PINS: A bodkin looks like a pair of tweezers and is used to thread elastic through casings. No bodkin? No problem. A safety pin is just as effective. Simply secure one end of the elastic on the bodkin or through the safety pin needle and thread through the casing, making sure that the unsecured end doesn't get lost in the casing.

SEAM RIPPER: A vital tool.

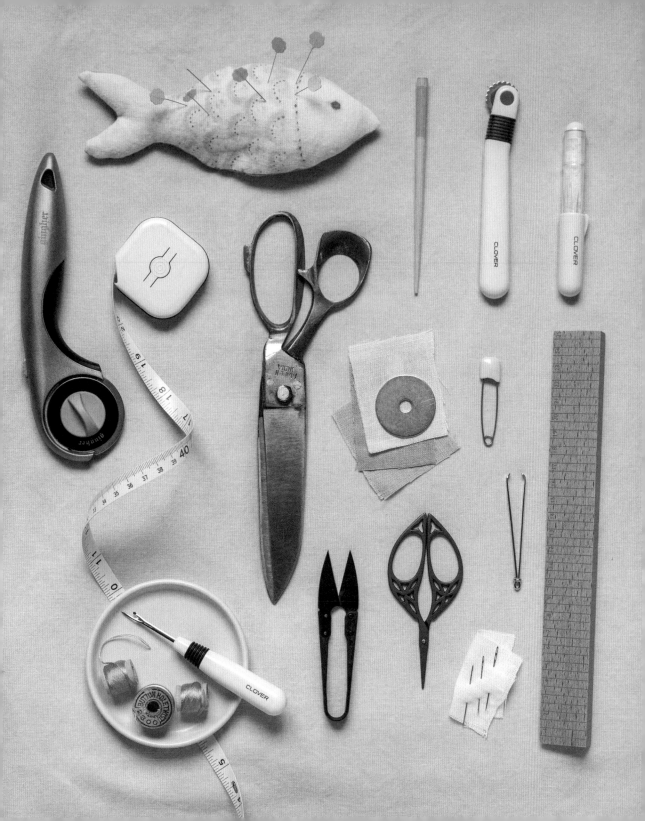

CUTTING TOOLS

The adage "measure twice and cut once" is one to live and die by when it comes to sewing.

FABRIC SHEARS: A bent-handle pair of fabric shears is well worth the investment. Always make sure to cut only fabric with your shears, as paper will dull them in a nanosecond.

ROTARY CUTTER: The razor-sharp, rotating blades are especially ideal for cutting straight lines along the edge of a ruler on a cutting mat. Nowadays there are models with smaller blades that better accommodate cutting around curves.

CUTTING MAT: Look for these self-healing mats in the largest size you can afford because they will become indispensable. Not only are they essential when using your rotary cutter, but also the ruled grid makes measuring fabrics a cinch. The cutting mat surface also keeps the fabric from shifting around.

QUILTING RULER: You've probably seen these see-through rulers around. An 18-inch quilting ruler is great for drafting patterns, marking lines, and using the rotary cutter.

MARKING TOOLS: There are so many marking tools available, and some of my favorites include ones with disappearing ink (there are also water-soluble and heat-disappearing types—you spray water on or iron the fabric and the ink disappears) and the Chaco Liner Pen Style chalk marker, which makes very precise markings. You will need a marking tool for every project in this book.

PATTERN WEIGHTS: Metal washers of varying sizes make effective pattern weights. They work fabulously for holding pattern pieces in place on fabric while tracing around them. Use them individually or stacked (the slipperier the fabric, the more weights I use).

PRESSING TOOLS

A proper ironing—or "pressing" in sewing lingo—can make a massive difference in the outcome of a project. Pressing isn't simply for smoothing out wrinkles; it also ensures accurate stitching and reinforces the shape of a sewn item.

IRON: These days there are irons that look like they could fly and communicate with satellites, but a basic model that has a steam option and a few heat settings is more than enough. Keep in mind that you are, in fact, pressing with the iron and not gliding it back and forth over the fabric. Firmly place your iron in the desired spot, hold for a few seconds, then slide to an adjacent spot and hold again.

IRONING BOARD: A traditional ironing board is handy, though any tabletop or flat surface will quickly convert to an ironing board with a thick, heat-resistant mat. You could even build your own customized ironing station with some plywood, batting, and heat-resistant fabric.

SEAM GAUGE: These small metal rulers are used to measure hems and folded edges of fabric. They're the kind with a little plastic slider to help you with various seam allowances too.

PRESS CLOTH: Synthetic mesh press cloths or organza work well because you can see through them. Be careful with the heat setting with the mesh press cloth. It's meant to protect the fabric you are ironing, but it may melt.

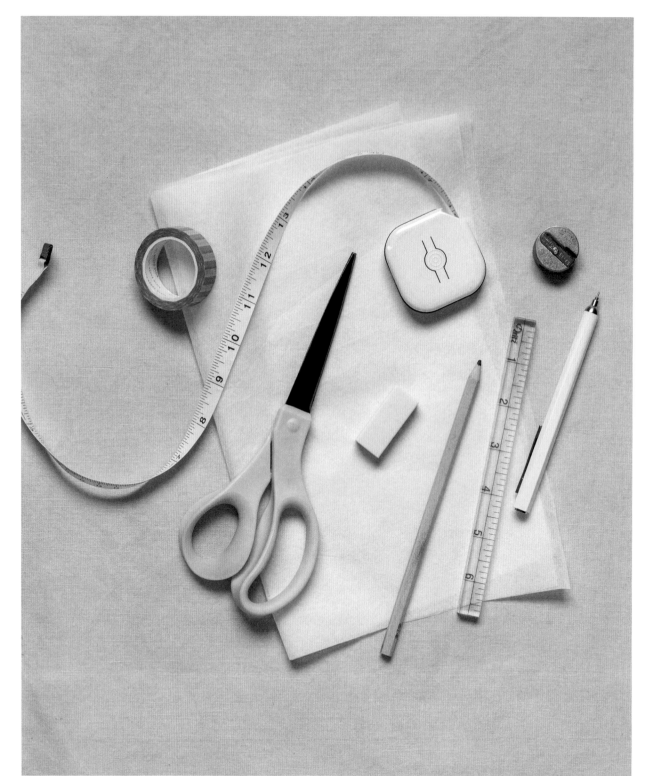

THE DRAFTING KIT

Traceable templates are provided for many of the projects in this book, but some will call for a "drafting kit," which is my fancy way of saying you'll need some paper, a ruler, and a writing utensil to draw your own pattern pieces. Following is a list of items that will make drafting super easy:

PATTERN PAPER: My tried-and-true paper is called Swedish tracing paper, which is a white, slightly sheer, durable, and sewable material. However, any large pieces or rolls of paper—kraft, butcher, drawing—will do the job.

PENCIL: I like to use mechanical pencils, but any pencil is great.

ERASER: You may end up erasing a lot of your lines, or you might be comfy leaving multiple sketched lines as is.

PEN: Unless I label my pattern pieces, I forget what they're for about a minute after I've drawn them. You could certainly use the pencil to label your pattern pieces when they're ready to go, but there's something official about using a pen.

RULER: I give my 18- and 24-inch quilting rulers quite a workout when it comes to drafting pattern pieces, but feel free to use any kind of ruler. For extra-long lines (see Drafting Hood + Cape Templates on page 153), a yardstick would be beneficial.

TAPE MEASURE: Made from fabric or vinyl, this tool is for measuring bodies and other three-dimensional objects. You could use a tape measure instead of a ruler to draft pattern pieces as well.

SCISSORS: Designate a separate pair of scissors just for cutting out pattern pieces (remember, your fabric shears should never touch paper!).

TAPE: Tape is useful when modifying pattern pieces or when you need to tape together paper for a larger surface area to create patterns.

RECOMMENDED FABRICS

There are no strict rules when it comes to fabrics for sewing projects, and in fact, it's that very freedom that makes sewing so creative and fun. The same project can look entirely different depending on the fabric you use. Here's a list of my most frequently recommended fabrics:

COTTON: Easy to sew, plentifully available, and infinite in variety, it's pretty hard to go wrong with cotton. This all-purpose fabric will work well for most of the projects in this book.

FAUX FUR: Given that this book is animal-themed, faux fur was bound to be featured. I especially like using Sherpa for the Sheep Backpack (page 163) and Beanies with Ears (page 125). For the beanie, make sure to select an extra-stretchy kind of faux fur.

FAUX LEATHER: Faux leather has come a long way, and you'd be hard-pressed to tell it apart from the genuine stuff. This unique fabric gives the Wall Pockets (page 73) extra visual interest. It's a little tricky to sew, but if you go slow you shouldn't have any problems.

GAUZE: I used light and airy gauze to line the Terry Cloth Bath Puppets (page 100).

KNITS/STRETCH FABRICS: Knits can range in drape, weight, texture, and substrate content like all fabrics, but their versatility is second to none. Bonus: the edges don't fray. The main differentiator between wovens (such as linen, cotton, and double gauze) and knits is that knit fabrics stretch. Using a zigzag stitch and sewing machine needles designed for stretch fabrics (see page 35) is highly recommended.

LINEN: I just can't get enough of this beautifully textured fabric woven from the fibers of the flax plant.

TERRY CLOTH: I love the classic slubby towel terry cloth, but French terry, which is almost like sweatshirt material, is also delightful.

WOOL FELT: Wool felt is thicker, more durable, and much lovelier than the ubiquitous polyester kind. Consider using it for the noses of the animal pillows (page 55) and to increase the quality of the Quiet Adventures Felt Book (page 109).

HANDY TERMS + TECHNIQUES

Sewing can often feel overwhelming with the zillions of stitches and techniques available. In this section, I've rounded up the basics. The following isn't intended to be a comprehensive guide to sewing but a highlight reel of things to keep in mind as you start on the projects. For more intensive sewing instruction, check out the books listed in Resources on page 221.

BACKSTITCHING: Though it's not called out in every project, you will be backstitching at the start and end of a seam. This means that you will sew a few stitches, then select your back button (or pull or lever or whatever functionality for reversing that your machine is equipped with) to sew backward over the first few stitches you created (or the last few if you are indeed at the end). I normally backstitch four or five stitches, and you can consider this step the equivalent of tying a knot to secure it. Otherwise, your stitches will unravel and your hard work will be for naught.

BASTE: A baste stitch holds pieces of fabric together temporarily. This can be done with a lengthened machine stitch or with a running stitch by hand.

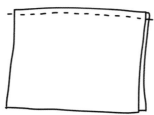

EDGESTITCH: This type of stitching is at the very edge of the fold of a fabric, usually ⅛ inch or less from the edge. It is often meant to be decorative, but in my projects, edgestitching is more often utilized as reinforcement or to close up openings from which pieces are turned right side out.

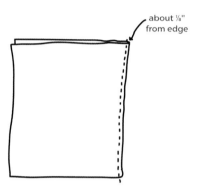

about ⅛"
from edge

FABRIC PREPARATION: Make sure to prewash and dry all fabrics. You will also want to iron/press the fabric before you begin drafting or tracing patterns onto the fabric. The exception to this general rule would be fabrics like faux leather, faux fur, and wool felt.

FINISHING: Fabrics such as cotton and linen will fray, so to prevent fabric edges from unraveling and turning into an unwieldy mass of threads, they need to be "finished." This can be done in several ways, such as by zigzag stitching or by overlock stitching with a serger if you have one. Most of the projects in this book will enclose the raw edges, so not a lot of finishing is required and zigzag stitching will suffice. Some textiles recommended in this book will not fray, including knits, wool felt, and faux leather.

GRAINLINE: The grainline will guide you when cutting out pattern pieces from fabric. The straight grain is parallel to the selvage (see page 47). The cross grain is perpendicular to the straight grain. And cutting on the bias means cutting diagonally, at a 45-degree angle. Think of it as a tic-tac-toe grid. The vertical lines are straight grain, the horizontal lines are cross grain, and if you get three X's in a diagonal row, it's a bias grain. The template pieces are marked with straight grain lines when appropriate.

I determine the grainline by what I call the "pull test." I tug at a piece of fabric to see which side stretches more. If I pull up and down and it stretches more than side to side, then I know that the side to side is parallel to the selvage. And vice versa. So the side that stretches less is parallel to the selvage.

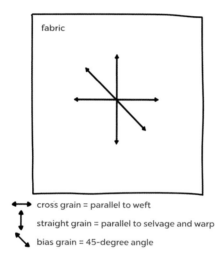

fabric

⟷ cross grain = parallel to weft

↕ straight grain = parallel to selvage and warp

↘ bias grain = 45-degree angle

RIGHT SIDE/WRONG SIDE: The "right side" (RS) refers to the outer-facing side of the fabric, and the "wrong side" (WS) is the interior-facing side of the fabric. Sometimes it's pretty obvious, but there are times when a fabric looks identical on both sides. In such cases, I recommend using your marking tool to indicate which side is the wrong side to make assembling the pieces easier down the line.

SATIN STITCH: The technique of attaching a piece of fabric on the right side of another piece of fabric is called appliqué, which can be achieved by hand-stitching or using a close-together zigzag stitch called a "satin stitch" with your sewing machine. I usually increase the stitch width to about 4 mm and reduce the stitch length to about 0.5 mm. In the illustration below, the lion face is satin-stitched onto the mane.

SEAM ALLOWANCE: The seam allowance is the section of fabric between the stitching line and the edge of the fabric when at least two pieces of material are sewn together. The seam allowance will vary across and within each project, so I've made sure to include the specific seam allowance information in each step. It is phrased as "sew ⅛ inch from the raw edge" or as "sew with a ⅛-inch seam allowance."

SELVAGE: Selvage is the nonfraying edge of a piece of fabric that runs parallel to what's called the warp. When you buy fabric, it's the section of the fabric with the brand and designer information printed on a thin strip along one edge. You can see that it doesn't unravel at all. The warp comprises threads that run longitudinally—in other words, vertically or up and down—and the weft comprises the threads that are woven in and out between the warp threads. See the illustration under Grainline (page 45).

SLIP STITCH: Many of the projects reference slip-stitching by hand to close openings in a seam. You will start by double knotting the end of your thread and inserting your needle from the underside of one opening edge to hide the knot. Pull the needle all the way through and pick up a few threads in the fabric directly across from where you pulled out your needle. Then pick up a few threads from the other side, inserting the needle from under the seam slightly away from the original stitch. Continue stitching this way until the opening is closed. Knot the thread, then insert the needle and pull out about a half inch from the insertion point to hide the knot. Clip the thread.

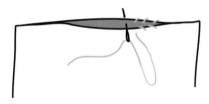

TOPSTITCH: Decorative or functional, topstitching is a line of stitching sewn from the right side of the fabric.

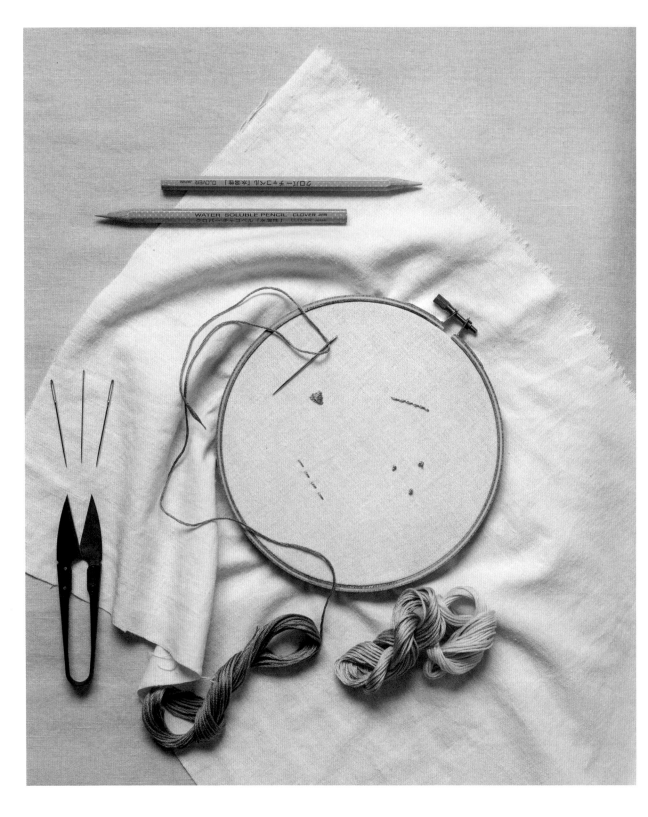

Embroidery Basics

I ABSOLUTELY LOVE HOW CHARMING HAND-STITCHING can be, especially with the imperfections. It's why the Japanese Sashiko-style embroidery has always appealed to me. All you need to know is the running stitch! In this book, I incorporated decorative Sashiko stitches for some projects and chose to embroider the eyes and nose of many of the animal faces. Feel free to do the same or skip the embroidery altogether and simply use buttons for eyes and wool felt for noses. I've listed some helpful supplies and stitching techniques below for those new to embroidery.

SUPPLIES

EMBROIDERY THREAD (OR FLOSS): Available in every hue imaginable, standard floss comes with six cotton strands twisted together. I typically use three or four strands, and you can separate the strands by pulling them apart gently.

EMBROIDERY NEEDLE: Embroidery needles are slightly thicker and have a larger needle eye compared with a regular hand-sewing needle.

WOODEN HOOP: Confession: I never use one. I have several and I'm sure they're handy, but I've found that I have no problems stitching directly on the fabric. I rather like the slightly askew, *wabi-sabi* results that I get.

MARKING TOOL: You might be super confident to go freehand, but I find it useful to mark where embroidered elements will be stitched onto the fabric.

SMALL SCISSORS: Try to use extra-sharp ones.

EMBROIDERY STITCHES

BACKSTITCH: Backstitching is the workhorse of embroidery and provides a continuous line of even stitches. It's basically the same idea as machine backstitching but done by hand in the case of embroidery. Backstitching is best for whiskers and for forming the outlines of eyes and nose shapes. Start by bringing the needle up at point A, then insert at point B and pull up from point C. To create the next stitch, insert the needle at point A, then pull up from point D.

FRENCH KNOT: A French knot can be used for little eyes or speckles on snouts and other decorative details. First, pull the needle up from point A. Holding the thread taut, wrap the floss around the needle twice. With the wrapped floss intact, insert the needle back into point A, and you should have a beautiful French knot.

SASHIKO: Similar to a gathering or basting stitch, Sashiko stitching is essentially a line of running stitches. Typically, the Sashiko stitches have a 3:2 ratio, which means that the stitches on the visible side are longer than they are on the bottom.

SATIN STITCH: Also known as a damask stitch, the satin stitch is great for covering a section of fabric with a series of flat stitches. I use the satin stitch method for the eyes and noses of animal faces. Narrow rows of satin stitching can also be created on a regular sewing machine using a zigzag stitch or special satin stitch foot. The zigzag method is how certain elements are appliquéd on some of the projects. To embroider with a satin stitch, start by making a small stitch, then pull up from point A and insert the needle at point B. Pull up at point C and insert at point D. Repeat until the section is covered.

STARTING AND ENDING WITHOUT A KNOT

A lot of embroidery projects recommend starting and ending a segment of stitching without a knot. I've illustrated this method below, but since all of the projects in this book will hide the back of the fabric, feel free to use a knot if it's easier for you.

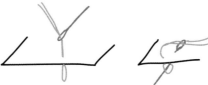

Project Instructions

|||||||||||||||||||||||||||||||||||||||||||

DECOR

Pillows
Polar Bear 55 • Lion 59
Koala 62 • Bunny 65 • Sloth 68

Placemats
Cat, Bear 70

Wall Pockets
Zebra, Reindeer 73

Rope Baskets
Cat, Dog 76

|||||||||||||||||||||||||||||||||||||||||||

Pillows

IT'S LIKE A CUDDLY SAFARI every day with these darling little animal pillows scattered about the room. The possibilities are endless with a little variation in the embroidery and ear shapes (and some animals don't even have ears, which makes it extra easy), so experiment away!

Polar Bear

PATTERN PIECES

Head (cut 2) - draft

Ears (cut 4)—template (see page 176)

Snout (cut 2)—template (see page 178)

Nose (cut 1)—template (see page 178)

SUPPLIES + MATERIALS

⅓ yard white fabric for face, snout, and ears

Scrap of black fabric for nose (wool felt is an excellent choice)

Stuffing (cotton, wool, or fiberfill)

Marking tool such as chalk

Embroidery floss: black

Embroidery needle

Hand-sewing needle

Coordinating thread

Drafting kit (see page 41)

Buttons for eyes (optional)

⸻⸻⸻⸻⸻⸻⸻

RECOMMENDED FABRICS

Linen, linen/cotton blend, cotton, felted wool

⸻⸻⸻⸻⸻⸻⸻

FINISHED DIMENSIONS

9½ inches wide by 10½ inches high

CONSTRUCTION STEPS

1 Draft an oval shape for the head. Start by folding a 10-by-11-inch piece of paper into quarters. Position the paper so that the folded edges are on the left and bottom. Make a mark ½ inch from the left edge and another mark ½ inch from the bottom right edge. Draw a diagonal from corner to corner, then mark 5½ inches from the lower left edge along this diagonal line. Connect the three dots into a smooth curve, then cut along the curve. Note that the height is longer than the width so you will end up with an oval shape. Unfold the paper and position it with the long side vertical. For ear placement, place the ruler at an angle from the top of the center fold and adjust the ruler until the 4½-inch mark intersects the oval. Mark the ear placement position.

2 Trace the templates for the head, ears, snout, and nose onto the appropriate fabric and cut out the pieces.

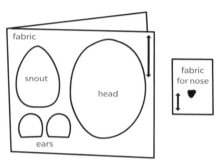

3 Make the snout. Sew right sides together with a ¼-inch seam allowance, leaving an opening of about 2 inches. Clip along the curved edge, making sure not to cut into the seam. Turn the snout right side out and press, folding the open edges inward. You do not need to close up the snout opening at this point; it will be closed later when the snout is attached to the face with a zigzag stitch.

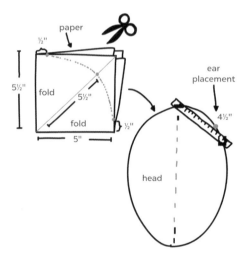

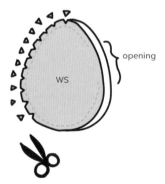

4 Make the nose and mouth. Appliqué the nose onto the right side of the snout piece with a satin/zigzag stitch, a little above the vertical midway point (see nose placement on the template). Because of the small size, feel free to hand-stitch if it feels easier. Alternatively, embroider the nose with black floss. Embroider the mouth with pink floss.

6 Embroider the eyes on the face piece. With a marking tool, determine the position of the eyes and mouth based on the illustration below. Embroider the eyes using a satin stitch (black floss). You could use buttons for eyes instead, if you prefer.

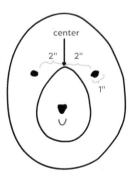

5 Appliqué the snout to the head. Using a satin/zigzag stitch on your machine, attach the snout to the head. We'll call this the face piece.

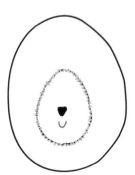

7 Make the ears. Sew each set of ear pieces with right sides together with a ¼-inch seam allowance along the curved edge. Do not sew the bottom edge. Trim the curved edges to about ⅛ inch. Turn right side out and press. Topstitch about ¼ inch from the edge, if desired. Align the raw edges, and with right sides together, baste the ears to the face piece where marked (the ears will be centered at marking).

8 Finish sewing the pillow. Sew the front and back head pieces with right sides together with a ⅜-inch seam allowance, leaving an opening of about 3 inches at the side, along one of the straighter edges. Clip the curves, making sure not to cut into the seam. Turn right side out and press.

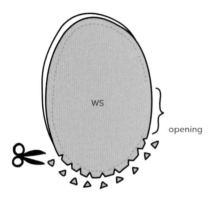

WS

opening

9 Stuff the pillow with small tufts of stuffing to avoid future bunching. Use plenty of stuffing until you get a nice rounded shape without straining the seams. I find a tool like a chopstick is helpful to get the stuffing into all the nooks and crannies. Slip-stitch the opening closed.

stuffing

Lion

PATTERN PIECES

Mane (cut 2)—draft

Face (cut 2)—template (see page 179)

Ears (cut 4)—template (see page 176)

Nose (cut 1)—template (see page 179)

CONSTRUCTION STEPS

1 Draft the mane. Start by folding a 12-by-11-inch piece of paper in half vertically. Draw a perpendicular line from the vertical center point (A). At about a 45-degree angle above and below the perpendicular line, plot 6-inch marks from point A. Using these points as a guide, draw curvy lines for the mane outline. Don't worry too much about symmetry or precision; you can always adjust the mane shape later. Draw an almost straight edge of about 3 inches near the bottom of the mane, where you can leave an opening that can later be closed easily with a slip stitch. Cut out the template.

SUPPLIES + MATERIALS

⅓ yard mustard or light brown fabric for mane

¼ yard beige fabric for face and ears

Scrap of black wool felt for nose

Stuffing (cotton, wool, or fiberfill)

Marking tool such as chalk

Embroidery floss: black, cream, pink, and mustard

Embroidery needle

Hand-sewing needle

Coordinating thread

Drafting kit (see page 41)

Buttons for eyes (optional)

||||||||||||||||||||||||||||||||||||||||||||

RECOMMENDED FABRICS

Linen, linen/cotton blend, cotton

||||||||||||||||||||||||||||||||||||||||||||

FINISHED DIMENSIONS

Approximately 11 inches wide by 10 inches high

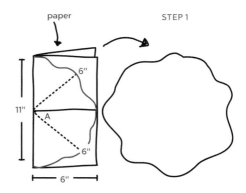

paper   STEP 1

2 Trace the templates for the mane, face, ears, and nose onto the appropriate fabric and cut out the pieces.

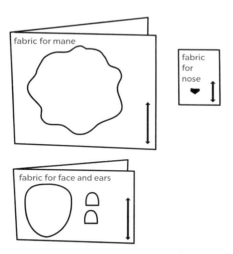

3 Make the ears. Sew each set of ear pieces with right sides together with a ¼-inch seam allowance along the curved edge. Do not sew the bottom edge. Trim the curved edges to about ⅛ inch. Turn right side out and press. Topstitch ¼ inch from curved edge, if desired. Align the raw edges, and baste the ears to the right side of one of the face pieces where marked. Make sure to center the ear pieces at the markings.

4 Make the face. Sew the front and back face pieces with right sides together with a ¼-inch seam allowance, leaving an opening of about 2 inches along one of the straighter edges. Clip along the curved edge, making sure not to cut into the seam. Turn right side out and press.

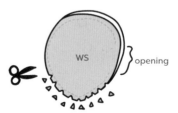

5 Make the nose, eyes, and mouth. Pin and satin/zigzag-stitch the nose onto the right side of the face piece with the basted ears (see the template for placement of the facial elements). Because of the small size, feel free to hand-stitch the nose if it feels easier. Use a marking tool to indicate the general positions of the eyes and mouth on the face piece. Embroider the eyes using a satin stitch (black floss) and the mouth using a backstitch (pink floss). You could also use buttons for eyes instead. With cream floss, add other decorative embroidery such as more nose definition and detailing on the forehead and whiskers, if desired.

6 Appliqué the face to the right side of one of the mane pieces by hand-stitching or using a machine satin/zigzag stitch. Press.

7 Make the mane. Embroider decorative running stitches that radiate outward from the face to the outer edge of the mane with mustard embroidery floss if desired. With right sides together, sew the front and back mane pieces with a ⅜-inch seam allowance, leaving an opening of about 3 inches at the bottom. Clip along the curved edge, making sure not to cut into the seam. Turn right side out and press.

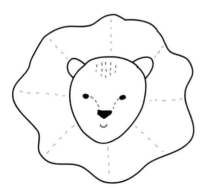

8 Stuff the pillow with small tufts of stuffing to avoid future bunching. Use plenty of stuffing until you get a nice rounded shape without straining the seams. I find a tool like a chopstick is helpful to get the stuffing into all the nooks and crannies. Slip-stitch opening closed.

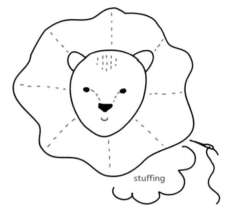

stuffing

Koala

PATTERN PIECES

Head (cut 2)—draft

Ears (cut 4)—template (see page 176)

Nose (cut 2)—template (see page 176)

CONSTRUCTION STEPS

1 Draft an oval shape for the head. Start by folding an 11-by-10-inch piece of paper into quarters. Position the paper so that the folded edges are on the left and bottom. Make a mark ½ inch from the top left edge and another mark ½ inch from the bottom right edge. Draw a diagonal from corner to corner, then mark 5½ inches from the lower left edge along this diagonal line. Connect the three dots into a smooth curve, then cut along the curve. Unfold the paper and position it with the long side horizontal. Note that the height is shorter than the width so you will end up with an oval shape. For ear placement, place the ruler at an angle from the top of the center fold and adjust the ruler until the 5-inch mark intersects the oval. Mark the ear placement position.

SUPPLIES + MATERIALS

⅓ yard gray fabric for face and ears

Scrap of black fabric for nose

Stuffing (cotton, wool, or fiberfill)

Marking tool such as chalk

Embroidery floss: black

Embroidery needle

Hand-sewing needle

Coordinating thread

Drafting kit (see page 41)

Buttons for eyes (optional)

RECOMMENDED FABRICS

Linen, linen/cotton blend, cotton, felted wool

FINISHED DIMENSIONS

16 inches wide by 9 inches high

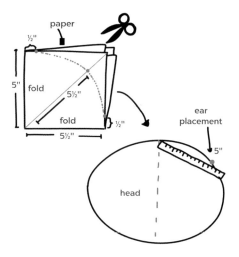

2 Trace the templates for the face, ears, and nose onto the appropriate fabric and cut out the pieces.

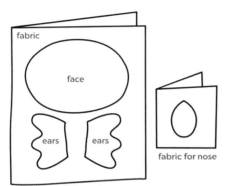

3 Make the nose. With right sides together, sew the nose pieces with a ¼-inch seam allowance, leaving an opening of about 1½ inches. Clip the tip of the nose and trim the seam allowance to about ⅛ inch except at the opening. Turn the nose right side out and press. Attach to the right side of one of the head pieces with a slip stitch (alternatively, appliqué using a satin/zigzag stitch with your sewing machine). I like to fold the head piece in half horizontally and then vertically to figure out where the center of the face is (where the two lines cross), but you could eyeball it for a more *wabi-sabi* look.

STEP 3

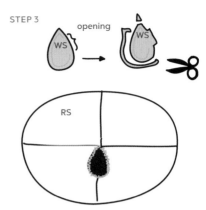

4 Embroider the eyes and mouth on the face piece, using a satin stitch for the eyes and a backstitch for the mouth (refer to page 50). With a marking tool, determine the positions for the eyes and mouth based on the illustration below, and embroider with black (for the eyes) and pink (for the mouth) embroidery floss. You could also use buttons for eyes instead.

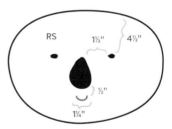

5 Make the ears. If desired, hand-sew decorative running stitches about ¾ inch from the curved edges on the right side of the left and right ears with black embroidery floss (I like to use three strands of floss). Sew each set of ear pieces with right sides together with a ¼-inch seam allowance along the curved edge. Do not sew the straight edge. Clip along the curved edges close to the seam but not into the seam. Turn right side out and press. Fill the ears with a bit of stuffing (they should still be fairly flat). I usually baste the straight edge closed about ¼ inch from the edge to avoid runaway stuffing, but that's entirely optional. Baste the ears to the front head piece (the side with the face) where marked.

6 Sew the front and back head pieces with right sides together with a ⅜-inch seam allowance, leaving an opening of about 3 inches at the bottom. Clip along the curved edge, making sure not to cut into the seam. Turn right side out and press.

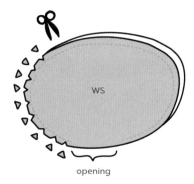

opening

7 Stuff the pillow with small tufts of stuffing to avoid future bunching. Use plenty of stuffing until you get a nice rounded shape without straining the seams. I find a tool like a chopstick is helpful to get the stuffing into all the nooks and crannies. Slip-stitch the opening closed.

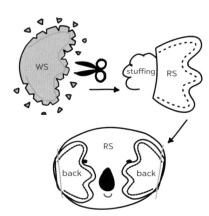

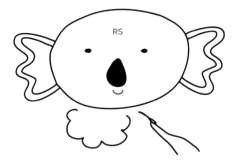

Bunny

PATTERN PIECES

Head (cut 2)—draft

Ears (cut 2 out of outer fabric and 2
   out of inner/lining fabric)—template
   (see page 177)

CONSTRUCTION STEPS

1 Draft an oval shape for the head. Start
by folding an 11-by-10-inch piece of
paper into quarters. Position the paper
with the folded edges on the left and
bottom. Make a mark ½ inch from the
top left edge and another mark ½ inch
up from the bottom right edge. Draw a
diagonal from corner to corner, then mark
5½ inches from the lower left edge along
this diagonal line. Connect the three dots
into a smooth curve, then cut along the
curve. Unfold the paper and position it
with the long side horizontal. Note that
the height is shorter than the width so
you will end up with an oval shape. For
ear placement, place the ruler at an angle
from the top of the center fold and adjust
the ruler until the 2½-inch mark intersects
the oval. Mark the ear placement position.

SUPPLIES + MATERIALS

⅓ yard sky blue fabric for head and ears

Scrap of white fabric for inner ears

Stuffing (cotton, wool, or fiberfill)

Marking tool such as chalk

Embroidery floss: black, pink, and white

Embroidery needle

Hand-sewing needle

Coordinating thread

Drafting kit (see page 41)

Buttons for eyes (optional)

RECOMMENDED FABRICS

Linen, linen/cotton blend, cotton

FINISHED DIMENSIONS

10 inches wide by 9 inches high, plus
ears are approximately 7½ inches long

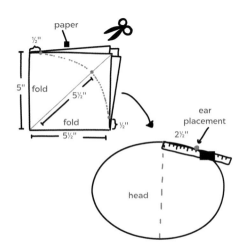

2. Trace the templates for the head and ears onto the appropriate fabric and cut out the pieces.

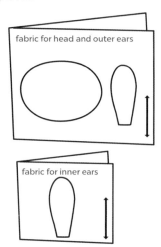

fabric for head and outer ears

fabric for inner ears

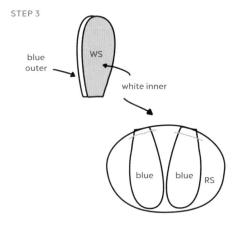

blue outer

WS

white inner

blue   blue   RS

3. Make the ears. Sew each set of ear pieces with right sides together with a ¼-inch seam allowance along the curved edge. Each ear should have one white piece and one sky blue piece. Do not sew the bottom edge. Clip along the curved edge, making sure not to cut into the seam. Turn right side out and press. Topstitch ¼ inch from the curved edge on the white side. Fill lightly with stuffing. With the white side facing down, align the raw edges and baste the ears to the right side of one of the head pieces where marked (you will center the ear pieces where marked). This will now be your front face piece, ready for embroidery.

4. Make the eyes, nose, and whiskers. Use a marking tool to indicate the general positions of the eyes, nose, and whiskers on the face piece based on the illustration below. Embroider the eyes (black floss) and nose (pink floss) using a satin stitch and the whiskers (white floss) using a backstitch. Use buttons for the eyes instead, if you prefer.

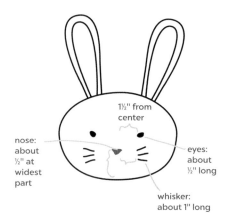

1½" from center

nose: about ½" at widest part

eyes: about ½" long

whisker: about 1" long

5 Finish sewing the head. Sew the front and back head pieces with right sides together with a ⅜-inch seam allowance, leaving an opening of about 3 inches at the bottom. Be careful not to accidentally sew the ears. Clip along the curved edge, making sure not to cut into the seam. Turn right side out and press.

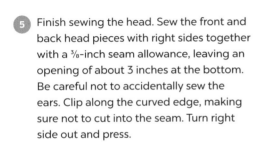
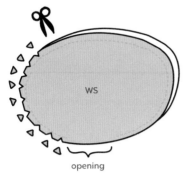

opening

6 Stuff the pillow with small tufts of stuffing to avoid future bunching. Use plenty of stuffing until you get a nice rounded shape without straining the seams. I find a tool like a chopstick is helpful to get the stuffing into all the nooks and crannies. Slip-stitch opening closed.

stuffing

Sloth

PATTERN PIECES

Head (cut 2)—draft

Eye patches (cut 2)—template (see page 180)

Face (cut 1)—template (see page 180)

CONSTRUCTION STEPS

1. Draft an oval shape for the head. Start by folding an 11-by-10-inch piece of paper into quarters. Position the paper so that the folded edges are on the left and bottom. Make a mark $\frac{1}{2}$ inch from the top left edge and another mark $\frac{1}{2}$ inch from the bottom right edge. Draw a diagonal from corner to corner, then mark $5\frac{1}{2}$ inches from the lower left edge along this diagonal line. Connect the three dots into a smooth curve, then cut along the curve. Note that the height is shorter than the width so you will end up with an oval shape. Unfold the paper and position it with the long side horizontal.

SUPPLIES + MATERIALS

$\frac{1}{3}$ yard beige fabric for head and eye patches

Scrap of white fabric for face

Stuffing (cotton, wool, or fiberfill)

Marking tool such as chalk

Embroidery floss: black and pink

Embroidery needle

Hand-sewing needle

Coordinating thread

Drafting kit (see page 41)

Buttons for eyes (optional)

RECOMMENDED FABRICS

Linen, linen/cotton blend, cotton, felted wool

FINISHED DIMENSIONS

10 inches wide by 9 inches high

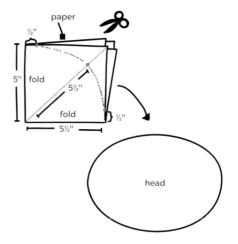

2 Trace the templates for the head, eye patches, and face onto the appropriate fabrics and cut out the pieces.

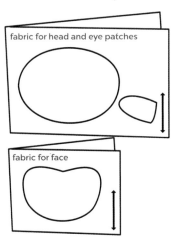

fabric for head and eye patches

fabric for face

3 Make the face. Use a satin/zigzag stitch to attach an eye patch on either side of the face piece at the markings. The eye patches should angle upward toward the center. Then satin/zigzag stitch the face piece to the right side of one of the head pieces. Press.

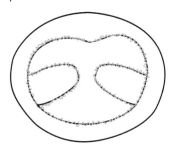

4 Make the eyes, nose, and mouth. Use a marking tool to indicate the general positions of the eyes, nose, and mouth on the face piece (see the template for placement positions). Embroider the eyes and nose using a satin stitch (black floss) and the mouth using a backstitch (pink floss). Use buttons for the eyes instead, if you prefer.

STEP 4

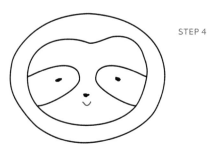

5 Finish sewing the head. With right sides together, sew the front and back head pieces with a ⅜-inch seam allowance, leaving an opening of about 3 inches at the bottom. Clip along the curved edge, making sure not to cut into the seam. Turn right side out and press.

opening

6 Stuff the pillow with small tufts of stuffing to avoid future bunching. Use plenty of stuffing until you get a nice rounded shape without straining the seams. I find a tool like a chopstick is handy to get the stuffing into all the nooks and crannies. Slip-stitch opening closed.

stuffing

Placemats

ELEVATE MEALTIMES WITH THESE MINIMALIST placemats. There's a pointy-ear version and a rounded-ear version—play a guessing game with little ones as to what kind of animals they could be! The small pocket is a handy place for utensils, napkins, a sweet note, or even small toys.

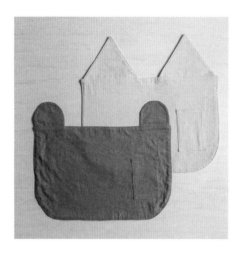

PATTERN PIECES

Face (cut 2)—draft

Pocket (cut 1)—draft

Ears (cut 4)—template (see page 181)

SUPPLIES + MATERIALS

Approx. ½ yard fabric per placemat

Coordinating thread

Marking tool such as chalk

Hand-sewing needle

Drafting kit (see page 41)

Interfacing (optional)

Point turner

୲୲୲୲୲୲୲୲୲୲୲୲୲୲୲୲୲୲୲୲୲୲୲୲୲୲୲୲୲୲

RECOMMENDED FABRICS

Linen, linen/cotton blends, cotton, canvas

୲୲୲୲୲୲୲୲୲୲୲୲୲୲୲୲୲୲୲୲୲୲୲୲୲୲୲୲୲୲

FINISHED DIMENSIONS

15½ inches wide by 14 inches high (including ears)

CONSTRUCTION STEPS

1 Make the pattern pieces. Measure out and cut (or tape together) a piece of paper that is 16 inches wide and 11 inches high. Fold the paper in half, mark 3 inches vertically and horizontally from the lower right corner on the unfolded side, and draw a curved line between the two points. Cut along the curve. Now you have the template for the main section of the placemat. For the pocket, cut out a rectangle that is 4 inches wide by 5½ inches high from another piece of paper. Place the pattern pieces on fabric and cut the pieces for the placemat and pocket. Feel free to measure and mark directly on the fabric, if it's easier for you.

STEP 1

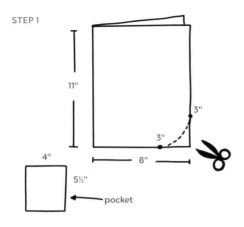

11"

3"

3"

4"

8"

5½"

pocket

2 Use the template to cut out the ears. For the triangles, I like to mark the bottom to avoid confusion later.

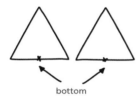

bottom

3 If you desire, iron on interfacing to the wrong side of the back pieces of the placemat and ear pieces to give them more structure.

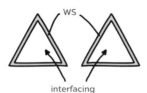

WS

interfacing

4 Make the ears. With right sides together and with a ¼-inch seam allowance, sew the ears around three sides, leaving the bottom open. Clip the corners (be careful not to cut into the seam!) and trim the seam allowance to about ⅛ inch. Turn right side out and push out the corners with point turner. Press, then topstitch ¼ inch from the edge.

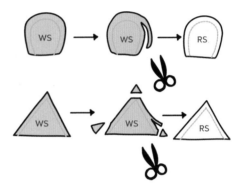

WS → WS → RS

WS → WS → RS

5 Attach ears to face. With right sides together, align the raw edges and baste the ears to the top of the front placemat piece, leaving ⅜ inch on each end. Note: the following illustrations will show pointy ears only, but the construction steps are the same for both types of ears.

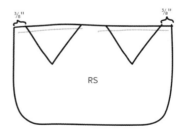

⅜" ⅜"

RS

6 To prepare the pocket, press three of the pocket sides ⅜ inch toward the wrong side and press. Fold the top toward the wrong side by ⅜ inch twice and press. Edgestitch the top of the pocket along the lower fold.

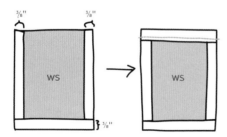

7 On the right side of the front placemat piece, pin the pocket 2 inches from the right edge and 3 inches from the bottom. Sew ⅛ inch from the edge of the pocket on three sides.

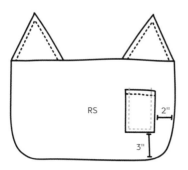

8 With right sides together, sew the front and back of the placemat with a ⅜-inch seam allowance, leaving an opening of about 3 inches at the bottom. Clip the corners and along the curved edges, turn right side out, and press.

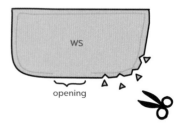

9 Topstitch ⅛ inch from the edge all around the face and close the opening.

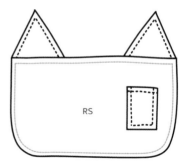

Wall Pockets

THIS ZEBRA OR REINDEER WALL pocket is a slight twist on taxidermy decor, and it's functional too: it's a great place to store art supplies or treasures from a nature walk. Replace the metal D-ring with a longer piece of ribbon, rope, or string to hang on a doorknob instead of the wall.

PATTERN PIECES

Wall pocket (cut 1 out of outer fabric and 1 out of lining fabric)—template (see pages 182–183)

D-ring holder (cut 1)—draft

SUPPLIES + MATERIALS

Tape

⅓ yard outer fabric

⅓ yard lining fabric

Fusible interfacing (optional)

Coordinating thread

Sharpies (black and white)

2 pieces of 35-inch floral wire (for antlers)

1½-inch D-ring

Scrap of faux leather or fabric (for D-ring)

Hand-sewing needle or hot-glue gun

||||||||||||||||||||||||||||||||||||||||||

RECOMMENDED FABRICS

Faux leather or decor-weight canvas for outer fabric; linen or cotton for lining

||||||||||||||||||||||||||||||||||||||||||

FINISHED DIMENSIONS

6 inches wide by 10 inches high (including ears but not antlers)

CONSTRUCTION STEPS

1 Assemble the template for the wall pocket by taping the upper and lower pieces together. Fold the fabric in half, and trace the template on the fold. Cut out the pieces.

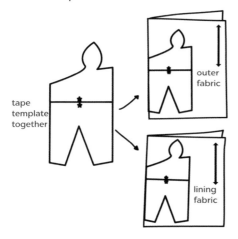

tape template together

outer fabric

lining fabric

STEP 2

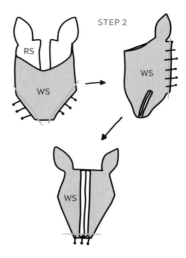

RS

WS

WS

WS

2 Assemble the outer piece. If using fabric that could use a little extra sturdiness, cut out a piece of interfacing using the outer piece template and fuse it onto the wrong side of the outer piece first. Sew the angled V section with right sides together with a ¼-inch seam allowance. With right sides together, sew the back center seam with a ¼-inch seam allowance. Press the seam allowance open (if using faux leather, finger-press it open). Then flatten the pocket and sew the bottom straight across with a ¼-inch seam allowance. Clip the corners and turn right side out. If using faux leather, finger-press to shape. For other fabrics, lightly press.

3 Make the D-ring holder. Cut out a piece of faux leather that is 1½ inches by 2½ inches. If using another type of fabric (i.e., fabric that frays) for the holder, cut a piece that is 2 inches by 3 inches. Fold, press the long edges to the wrong side, and edgestitch. Slip the D-ring in the middle, and fold in half with wrong sides together. Align the raw edge of the holder to the center right side of the outer wall pocket on the back side and baste.

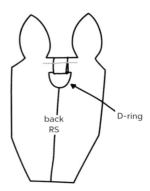

back RS

D-ring

4 Make the lining. Repeat step 2 for the wall pocket lining, but leave an opening of about 3 inches along the back center seam. Press the seam open.

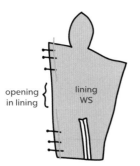

opening in lining

lining
WS

6 Using a Sharpie, draw the eyes and any other elements if desired. Refer to the illustration below for placement of facial elements.

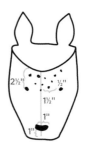

5 Attach the lining. Sew the wall pocket and lining right sides together with a ¼-inch seam allowance along the top edge and along the ears, tucking the D-ring between the lining and outer layers. Clip the corners and curves, making sure not to cut into the seam. Turn right side out from the lining opening and finger-press to shape. Slip-stitch the opening closed.

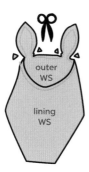

outer
WS

lining
WS

7 If adding antlers, form long, skinny loops out of floral wire and twist them into an antler shape. Attach to the back of the wall pocket by hand-sewing or using a hot-glue gun.

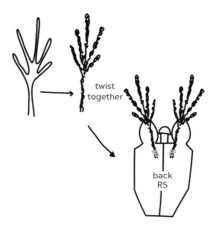

twist together

back
RS

Rope Baskets

IT'S SURPRISINGLY EASY AND SOOTHING to make these dog and cat rope baskets. Organizing is so much more rewarding with handcrafted containers!

SUPPLIES + MATERIALS

At least 100 feet rope (5 mm or 8 mm thickness in cotton will work best, and the standard clothesline rope is quite economical)

Coordinating thread (at least one 500-meter/547-yard spool of all-purpose polyester or cotton thread)

Thick sewing machine needle (denim or leather needles are recommended)

Embroidery floss (a contrasting color that will show up on the rope)

Embroidery needle

Marking tool

FINISHED DIMENSIONS

Approximately 28-inch circumference by 5 inches high (without ears; pointy ears add about 2 inches to height) by 8-inch-diameter base

TIP: Fill at least three bobbins in advance because you will be going through a lot of thread!

CONSTRUCTION STEPS

1 Begin the basket. Make sure to use a thicker sewing machine needle for this project, such as a denim or leather needle. Start by coiling one end of the rope into a small spiral and pin to secure if you find the rope to be slippery or fiddly. Place the small spiral under the presser foot, and using the widest zigzag stitch (mine is 5 mm), sew the spiral to secure. You don't have to be too precise at this stage, but make sure that the loose/extra rope is hanging off of the right side of the presser foot. This is very important!

2 Make the base. With the presser foot positioned where the two coils meet, zigzag-stitch around and around while pressing the rope gently together until you have a base that is about 8 to 9 inches. Be patient; this basket takes a while, but it's extremely meditative to make.

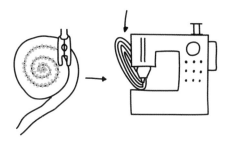

3 Make the sides. When the base is completed, start tipping the base toward the right as you sew until the base is at a 90-degree angle. You are now creating the side of the basket. Keep zigzag-stitching with the needle positioned right between the ropes until the side reaches a height of approximately 5 inches. Backstitch and take it out of the machine.

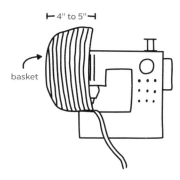

4 Mark the ear positions using pins. First, determine where the center front will be.

a. For pointy ears: Place two pins 5 inches apart at the front (2½ inches on each side of the center pin). Then measure 3 inches outward from each pin.

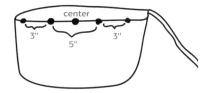

b. For floppy ears: Place two pins 7 inches apart at the front (3½ inches on each side of the center pin). Then measure 6 inches outward from each pin.

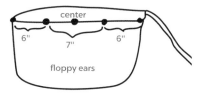

5 Make the ear handles. Place the basket back under the presser foot where you left off, making sure the rope is still hanging off to the right side. Sew up to the first outer pin, backstitch, then measure out 5 inches of rope (for pointy ears) or 8 inches of rope (for floppy ears) and resume sewing at the next pin until you reach the beginning of the second ear. Go slow here because it could be a little unwieldy. I find it easier to take the basket out once I've backstitched, measure out the rope, pin it to the next ear position, and then resume sewing (don't forget to backstitch). When you get to the next pin, measure out another 5 or 8 inches of rope, then resume sewing where the last pin is placed. You will sew the second row for the ears normally, without needing to pin, remove the basket, etc.

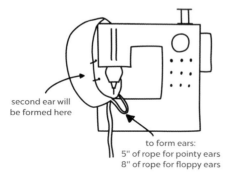

second ear will be formed here

to form ears:
5" of rope for pointy ears
8" of rope for floppy ears

6 Finish the basket. Sew up to the back center and slightly curve the rope down as you stitch about an inch, then cut the rope and backstitch several times to secure the end. Check the basket and zigzag-stitch to close up any missed spots. Note: Depending on the rope material, the pointy ears may tend toward floppiness. I used cotton clothesline rope and pinched them a bit with my fingers to achieve the pointedness.

7 Embroider the eyes, nose, and whiskers with embroidery floss, if desired. Using chalk or a marking tool, mark the nose and whisker positions (see illustration below for placement of facial elements). Refer to Embroidery Basics (page 51) on how to start and end without a knot. Embroider with a backstitch for the eyes and whiskers and a satin stitch for the nose.

same for both

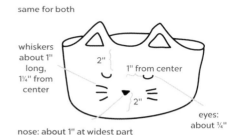

whiskers about 1" long, 1¼" from center

2"

1" from center

2"

eyes: about ¾"

nose: about 1" at widest part

Stackable Blocks

LINE THEM UP, STACK THEM UP, fling them in the air . . . oh, so many options! A fantastic way to develop hand-eye coordination, these soft fabric blocks are ideal for the crawling and toddling set.

Mouse

PATTERN PIECES

3-inch square (cut 6)—template (see page 186)

Ears (cut 4)—template (see page 187)

CONSTRUCTION STEPS

1 On the fabric, trace the templates for the square pieces and ears. Cut out all the pieces. Optional: cut out six square pieces of fusible interfacing and attach to the wrong side of each square piece.

SUPPLIES + MATERIALS

Approx. ¼ yard light gray fabric

Embroidery floss: black

Embroidery needle

Coordinating thread

Foam block* or stuffing (cotton, wool, or fiberfill)

Hand-sewing needle

Fusible interfacing (optional)

*Most fabric stores like JOANN will cut foam blocks to size if you request it. Or you can use a serrated knife or small saw to cut larger pieces of foam.

RECOMMENDED FABRICS

Linen, cotton/linen blend, cotton, twill, canvas, denim

FINISHED DIMENSIONS

2 inches by 2 inches by 2 inches (without ears; with ears, it's about 3½ inches high)

STEP 1

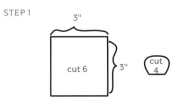

3"

cut 6

3"

cut 4

2 Make the ears. Sew the two sets of ears right sides together with a ¼-inch seam allowance. Clip the corners, trim the seam allowance to about ⅛ inch, turn right side out, and press. Baste onto the right side of one of the square pieces, ½ inch from each top corner.

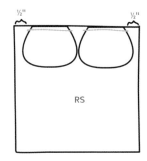

½"   ½"

RS

3 Embroider the eyes, nose, and whiskers. Referring to the template for placement of facial features, use a backstitch for the eyes and whiskers and a satin stitch for the nose.

4 Place a fabric square on top of the face with right sides together. Leaving ½ inch on each end, sew across one side with a ½-inch seam allowance. If you are sewing the top edge of the face, be careful not to stitch into the ear. Tip: making the ½-inch marks on all square corners before sewing makes it easier. Press the seam allowance open.

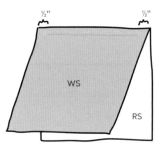

½"   ½"

WS

RS

5 Repeat step 4 with another fabric square, making sure to leave ½ inch unsewn on each end.

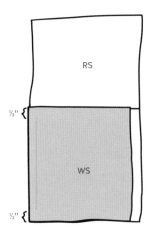

RS

½" {

WS

½" {

6 Repeat with the other two sides of the face.

7 Sew the last square piece to the topmost square piece with right sides together, making sure to leave ½ inch on each end. Press the seam allowances open, then press the edges along the folds from the right side to create sharp creases.

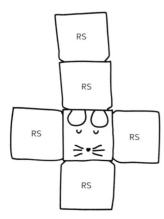

8 Sew the four squares surrounding the face with right sides together, making sure to leave ½ inch at each end. You may need to shift the corner sections out of the way as you sew the sides together. Avoid sewing into the ears.

STEP 8

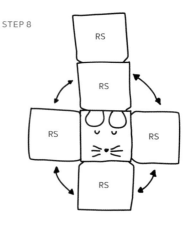

9 Sew two sides of the last square piece and leave one side open. Trim the corners, turn right side out, push out all the corners, and adjust the shape. Fold the edges of the opening toward the wrong side by ½ inch and press.

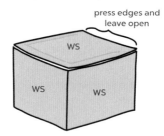

press edges and leave open

10 Insert the foam block or fill with stuffing. Slip-stitch the opening closed. Note: if using stuffing, the blocks will be a little more rounded compared with using foam blocks.

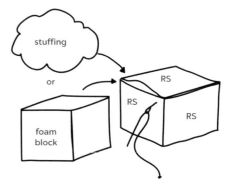

stuffing

or

foam block

Raccoon

PATTERN PIECES

4-inch square (cut 6)—template (see page 186)

Ears (cut 4)—template (see page 187)

Eye patches (cut 2)—template (see page 187)

CONSTRUCTION STEPS

1. On the beige fabric, trace the template for the square pieces; on the black fabric, trace the ear and eye patch templates. Cut out all the pieces. If you would like to reinforce the fabric, cut out six square pieces of fusible interfacing and attach to the wrong side of each square piece.

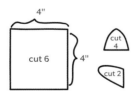

SUPPLIES + MATERIALS

Approx. ¼ yard beige fabric for block

Scrap of black fabric for ears and eye patches

Embroidery floss: black and white

Embroidery needle

Coordinating thread

Foam block* or stuffing (cotton, wool, or fiberfill)

Hand-sewing needle

Fusible interfacing (optional)

*Most fabric stores like JOANN will cut foam blocks to size if you request it. Alternatively, you can use a serrated knife or small saw to cut larger pieces of foam.

RECOMMENDED FABRICS

Linen, cotton/linen blend, cotton, twill, canvas, denim

FINISHED DIMENSIONS

3 inches by 3 inches by 3 inches (without ears; with ears, it's about 5 inches high)

2 Make the ears. Sew the two sets of ears right sides together with a ¼-inch seam allowance. Clip the corners, trim the seam allowance to about ⅛ inch, turn right side out, and press. Baste onto the right side of one of the square pieces, ½ inch from each top corner.

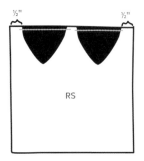

3 Make the eye patches. Satin/zigzag-stitch the black eye pieces to the right side of the square piece from step 2, about 1½ inch from the top edge.

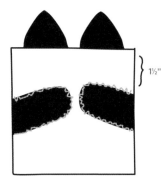

4 Embroider the eyes and nose. Referring to the template for placement of facial features, use a backstitch for the eyes (white floss) and a satin stitch for the nose (black floss).

STEP 4

5 Place a fabric square on top of the face with right sides together. Leaving ½ inch on each end, sew across with a ½-inch seam allowance. Tip: making the ½-inch marks on all square corners before sewing makes it easier. Press the seam allowance open.

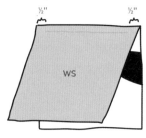

6 Repeat step 5 with another fabric square, making sure to leave ½ inch unsewn on each end.

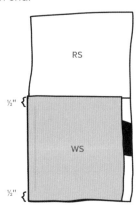

7 Repeat with the other two sides of the face.

start and stop ½" from each end

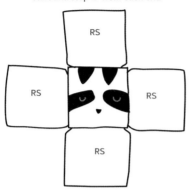

8 Sew the last square piece to the topmost square piece with right sides together, making sure to leave ½ inch on each end. Press the seam allowances open, then press the edges along the folds from the right side to create sharp creases.

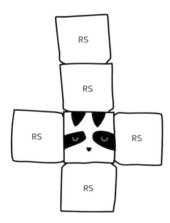

9 Sew the four squares surrounding the face with right sides together, making sure to leave ½ inch at each end. You may need to shift the corner sections out of the way as you sew the sides together.

STEP 9

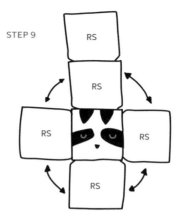

10 Sew two sides of the last square piece and leave one side open. Trim the corners, turn right side out, push out all the corners, and adjust the shape. Fold the edges of the opening toward the wrong side by ½ inch and press.

press edges and leave open

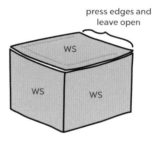

11 Insert the foam block or fill with stuffing. Slip-stitch the opening closed. Note: if using stuffing, the blocks will be a little more rounded compared with using foam blocks.

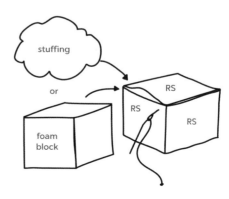

Bear

PATTERN PIECES

5-inch square (cut 6)—template (see page 184)

Ears (cut 4)—template (see page 187)

Snout (cut 1)—template (see page 187)

CONSTRUCTION STEPS

1 On the black fabric, trace the template for the square pieces and trace the ear template; on the gray fabric, trace the snout template. Cut out all the pieces. If you would like to reinforce the fabric, cut out six square pieces of fusible interfacing and attach to the wrong side of each square piece.

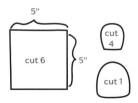

SUPPLIES + MATERIALS

Approx. ¼ yard black fabric for the block and ears

Scrap of gray fabric for the snout

Embroidery floss: black and white

Embroidery needle

Coordinating thread

Foam block* or stuffing (cotton, wool, or fiberfill)

Hand-sewing needle

Fusible interfacing (optional)

*Most fabric stores like JOANN will cut foam blocks to size if you request it. Alternatively, you can use a serrated knife or small saw to cut larger pieces of foam.

RECOMMENDED FABRICS

Linen, cotton/linen blend, cotton, twill, canvas, denim

FINISHED DIMENSIONS

4 inches by 4 inches by 4 inches (without ears; with ears, it's about 6 inches high)

2 Make the ears. Sew the two sets of ears right sides together with a ¼-inch seam allowance. Clip the corners, trim the seam allowance to about ⅛ inch, turn right side out, and press. Baste onto the right side of one of the square pieces, ½ inch from each top corner.

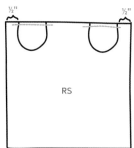

3 Make the snout. Satin/zigzag-stitch to the right side of the square piece from step 2, about 1 inch from the bottom.

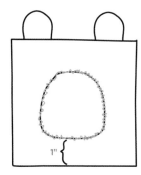

4 Embroider the eyes and nose. Referring to the template for placement of facial features, use a backstitch for the eyes (white floss) and a satin stitch for the nose (black floss).

5 Place a fabric square on top of the face with right sides together. Leaving ½ inch on each end, sew across with a ½-inch seam allowance. Tip: making the ½-inch marks on all square corners before sewing makes it easier. Press the seam allowance open.

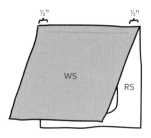

6 Repeat step 5 with another fabric square, making sure to leave ½ inch unsewn on each end.

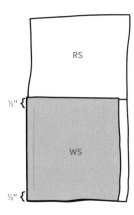

7 Repeat with the other two sides of the face.

start and stop ½" from each end

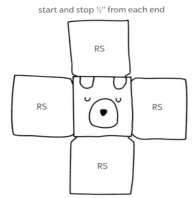

8 Sew the last square piece to the topmost square piece with right sides together, making sure to leave ½ inch on each end. Press the seam allowances open, then press the edges along the folds from the right side to create sharp creases.

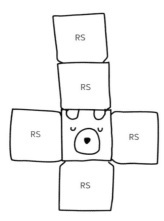

9 Sew the four squares surrounding the face with right sides together, making sure to leave ½ inch at each end. You may need to shift the corner sections out of the way as you sew the sides together.

STEP 9

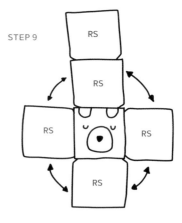

10 Sew two sides of the last square piece and leave one side open. Trim the corners, turn right side out, push out all the corners, and adjust the shape. Fold the edges of the opening toward the wrong side by ½ inch and press.

press edges and leave open

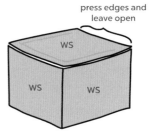

11 Insert the foam block or fill with stuffing. Slip-stitch the opening closed. Note: if using stuffing, the blocks will be a little more rounded compared with using foam blocks.

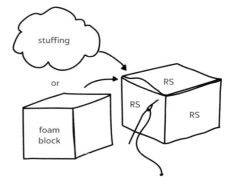

Elephant

PATTERN PIECES

6-inch square (cut 6)—template (see page 185)

Ears (cut 4)—template (see page 187)

Trunk (cut 2)—template (see page 187)

CONSTRUCTION STEPS

1 On the fabric, trace the templates. Cut out all the pieces. If you would like to reinforce the fabric, cut six square pieces of fusible interfacing and attach to the wrong side of each square piece.

SUPPLIES + MATERIALS

Approx. ¼ yard gray fabric

Embroidery floss: black

Embroidery needle

Coordinating thread

Foam block* or stuffing (cotton, wool, or fiberfill)

Hand-sewing needle

Fusible interfacing (optional)

*Most fabric stores like JOANN will cut foam blocks to size if you request it. Alternatively, you can use a serrated knife or small saw to cut larger pieces of foam.

RECOMMENDED FABRICS

Linen, cotton/linen blend, cotton, twill, canvas, denim

FINISHED DIMENSIONS

5 inches by 5 inches by 5 inches (not including ears; with ears, it's about 8½ inches long)

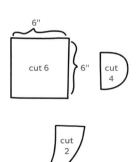

2. Make the ears. Sew the two sets of ears right sides together around the curved edge with a ¼-inch seam allowance, leaving the straight edge open. Clip the corners, trim the seam allowance to about ⅛ inch, turn right side out, and press. Baste onto each side of one of the square pieces (on the right side), ½ inch from the top edge.

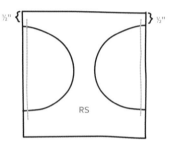

3. Make the trunk. Sew the trunk pieces right sides together with a ¼-inch seam allowance, leaving the straight edge open. Clip the corners, trim the seam allowance to about ⅛ inch, and turn right side out. Then fold in the top of the trunk by ¼ inch and press. Position the trunk on the face about 1½ inches from the top edge, and hand-sew or machine-stitch into place.

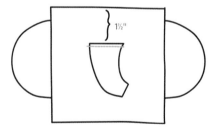

4. Embroider the eyes if desired. Referring to the template for placement of the eyes, use a backstitch.

STEP 4

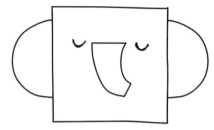

5. Place another square of fabric on top of the face with right sides together. Open out the ears to avoid accidentally sewing onto them. Leaving ½ inch on each end, sew across with a ½-inch seam allowance. Tip: making the ½-inch marks on all square corners before sewing makes it easier. Press the seam allowance open.

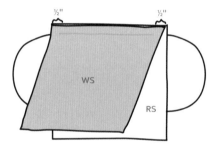

6. Repeat step 5 with another fabric square, sandwiching the left ear. Make sure to leave ½ inch unsewn on each end.

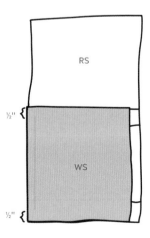

7 Repeat with the other two sides of the face.

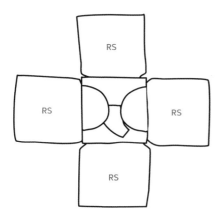

8 Sew the last square piece to the topmost square piece with right sides together, making sure to leave ½ inch on each end. Press the seam allowances open, then press the edges along the folds from the right side to create sharp creases.

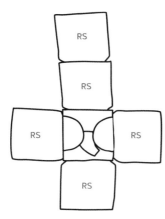

9 Sew the four squares surrounding the face with right sides together, making sure to leave ½ inch at each end. You may need to shift the corner sections out of the way as you sew the sides together. Avoid sewing into the ears.

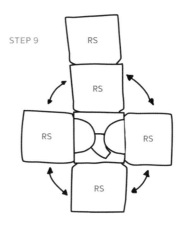

10 Sew two sides of the last square piece and leave one side open. Trim the corners, turn right side out, push out all the corners, and adjust the shape. Fold the edges of the opening toward the wrong side by ½ inch and press.

press edges and leave open

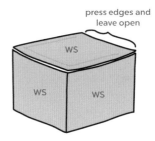

11 Insert the foam block or fill with stuffing. Slip-stitch opening closed. Note: if using stuffing, the blocks will be a little more rounded compared with using foam blocks.

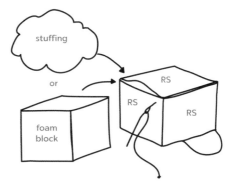

Teether Rattles

THIS TWOFER TOY IS A rattle *and* a teether. If you add short strips of ribbon and use fabrics with various textures, it can be a triple threat as a tactile toy as well.

Whale

PATTERN PIECES

Upper body (cut 2)—template
(see page 188)

Lower body (cut 2)—template
(see page 188)

Fin (cut 4)—template (see page 189)

Tail (cut 2)—template (see page 189)

SUPPLIES + MATERIALS

Approx. ¼ yard chambray fabric for
upper body, outer tail, and fins

Approx. ¼ yard gray fabric for lower
body (the fabric I used had a print
that looked like embroidery, but you
could embroider it yourself or skip
that entirely) and underside of tail

Embroidery floss: silver (optional)

Embroidery needle (optional)

Hand-sewing needle

Coordinating thread

5 inches of ribbon about ½ inch wide

Natural wood rings (I used 2¼-inch-
diameter rings)

Two ½-inch jingle bells

Stuffing (cotton, wool, or fiberfill)

RECOMMENDED FABRICS

Linen, cotton/linen blend, cotton

FINISHED DIMENSIONS

8½ inches wide by 3 inches high

CONSTRUCTION STEPS

1 Trace the templates for the upper body and fins onto the chambray fabric and for the lower body onto the gray fabric. Trace the tail onto the chambray and gray fabrics (you will need one tail piece per fabric). Cut out all the pieces.

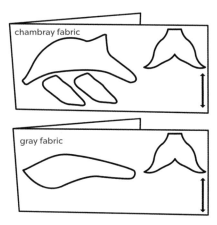

2 Make the lower body. If desired, embroider simple running stitches on both pieces. Sew the lower body pieces right sides together along the lower curve only with a ¼-inch seam allowance, leaving an opening of about 2 inches. Clip the curves without cutting into seam. Turn right side out and press.

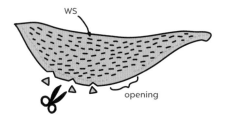

3 Make the fins. Sew the two sets of fins right sides together with a ¼-inch seam allowance. Trim the seam allowance to about ⅛ inch, turn right side out, press, and baste onto the right side of the lower body at the marking on the template. The marking should match the center of the fin.

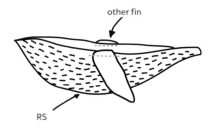

4 Add the wooden ring. Slip a piece of ribbon through the wooden ring, match the raw edges, and baste to the right side of one of the upper body pieces with a seam allowance slightly less than ¼ inch.

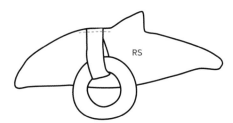

5 Make the upper body. Sew the pieces right sides together with a ¼-inch seam allowance along top edge only, sandwiching the ribbon with the wooden ring. Clip the corners and curves, making sure not to cut into the seam. Turn right side out, poking out all the parts with a pointy tool like a chopstick, and press.

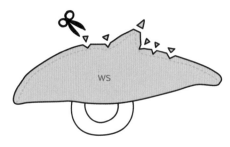

6 Assemble the body. With right sides together, sew the upper and lower body together with a ¼-inch seam allowance. You may have to stretch the fabric a little to get the two pieces to line up evenly. It also might be easier to have the wooden ring hanging out of the opening as you sew. Clip the corners and curves, turn right side out from the lower body opening, pushing out all the corners with a sharpish tool, and press.

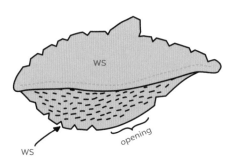

7 Sew the tail pieces right sides together with a ¼-inch seam allowance. Clip the corners, trim the seam allowance to about ⅛ inch, turn right side out, and press. There is no need to stuff the tail. Fold in the raw edge about ¼ inch and hand-sew to the end of the body.

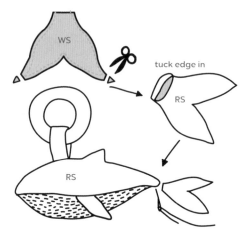

8 Fill the whale with stuffing, tucking in the jingle bells. Slip-stitch the opening closed.

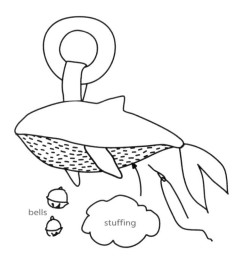

Dove

SUPPLIES + MATERIALS

Approx. ¼ yard natural linen or ivory fabric

Embroidery floss: gold

Embroidery needle

Hand-sewing needle

Coordinating thread

5 inches of ribbon about ½ inch wide

Natural wood rings (I used 2¼-inch-diameter rings)

Two ½-inch jingle bells

Stuffing (cotton, wool, or fiberfill)

ıııııııııııııııııııııııııııııııııı

RECOMMENDED FABRICS

Linen, cotton/linen blend, cotton

ıııııııııııııııııııııııııııııııııı

FINISHED DIMENSIONS

8 inches wide (with tail) by 4 inches high

PATTERN PIECES

Upper body (cut 2)—template (see page 190)

Stomach/bottom (cut 1)—template (see page 191)

Wings (cut 4)—template (see page 190)

CONSTRUCTION STEPS

1 Trace the templates onto the fabric and cut out all the pieces.

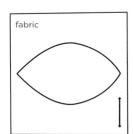

fabric

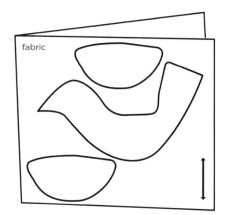

fabric

fabric

2 Add embroidery. If desired, embroider eyes and any other sections of the upper and lower pieces on both sides. Refer to the illustration below for placement of elements. Use a satin stitch for the eyes and running stitches for the embroidery on the tail. For a tactile, sensory toy version, attach folded pieces of ribbon and baste the unfolded side to the right side of the tail.

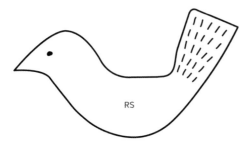

3 Attach the wooden ring. Slip a piece of ribbon through the wooden ring, match the raw edges, and baste to the right side of one of the top pieces where marked with a seam allowance slightly less than ¼ inch.

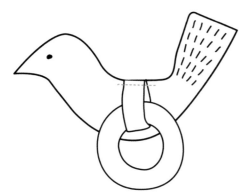

4 Sew the upper body. With right sides together, sew the pieces with a ¼-inch seam allowance, sandwiching the ribbon with the wooden ring. Refer to template for where to stop sewing. This is to accommodate the stomach/bottom piece. Clip the corners and curves, making sure not to cut into the seam. Turn right side out, poking out all the parts, and press.

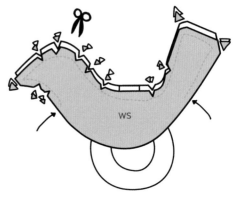

5 Sew the stomach/bottom. With right sides together, pin the upper body and stomach/bottom pieces right sides together, tucking the wooden ring inside. Use lots of pins; you may need to stretch the upper body a little to match up with the stomach/bottom section. Sew with a ¼-inch seam allowance, leaving an opening of about 2 inches along the side of the body on one side. Clip the corners and curves without cutting into the seam. Turn right side out from the opening, pushing out all the corners with a sharpish tool, and press.

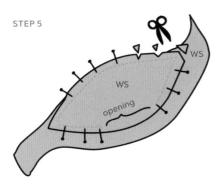

6 Fill with stuffing, tucking in the jingle bells. Slip-stitch the opening closed.

7 Make the wings. Embroider what will be the front sides of the left and right wings with running stitches. Another option for a tactile, sensory toy version is to attach folded pieces of ribbon and baste the unfolded side to the right side of the outer wing before sewing the wing pieces together. With right sides together, sew the wing pieces with a ¼-inch seam allowance, leaving an opening of about 2 inches at the top. Clip the curves without cutting into the seam, turn right side out, and press. Slip-stich a wing on each side of the bird.

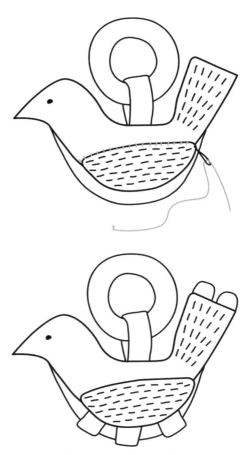

tactile/sensory version with ribbons

Bunny Ears

SUPPLIES + MATERIALS

Approx. ¼ yard pink outer fabric

Approx. ¼ yard gray lining fabric

Hand-sewing needle

Coordinating thread

5 inches of ribbon about ½ inch wide

Natural wood rings (I used 2¼-inch-
diameter rings)

Two ½-inch jingle bells

Stuffing (cotton, wool, or fiberfill)

RECOMMENDED FABRICS

Linen, cotton/linen blend, cotton

FINISHED DIMENSIONS

14 inches wide by 3 inches high

PATTERN PIECES

Ears (cut 1 from outer fabric, cut 1 from
lining)—template (see page 192)

CONSTRUCTION STEPS

1 Trace the template onto the fabrics and
cut out the pieces. You can either trace
two separate pieces on the fold or trace
one half of the template, then flip over
and trace the other half and cut two.
(See step 1 of the panda instructions on
page 101 for reference.)

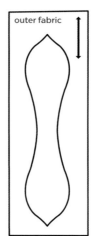

outer fabric

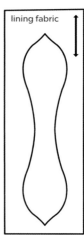

lining fabric

2 Sew the ear pieces. With right sides together, sew one pink piece and one gray piece with a ¼-inch seam allowance, leaving an opening of about 3 inches in the middle section.

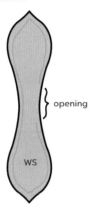

opening

WS

3 Fill the rattle. Clip the corners and curves without cutting into the seam, then turn right side out and press. Place a jingle bell in each ear. Topstitch ⅛ inch from edge, avoiding the bells.

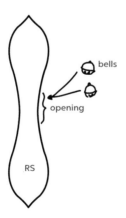

bells

opening

RS

4 Attach the ears to the wooden ring. Fold the piece in half and insert the folded part into the ring. Pull the ears through the folded loop and tighten. Stitch into place if desired to ensure the ears cannot be removed from the ring.

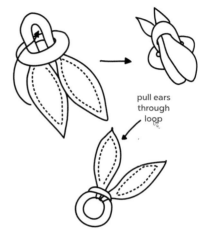

pull ears through loop

Terry Cloth Bath Puppets

NOT ONLY CAN THESE CRITTERS scrub all the grubbiness off, but they might also inspire an impromptu bath time puppet show!

Panda

PATTERN PIECES

Panda body (cut 2 from outer fabric, cut 2 from lining fabric)—template (see page 193)

Eyes (cut 2)—template (see page 193)

Ears (cut 4)—template (see page 193)

Arms (cut 4)—template (see page 193)

SUPPLIES + MATERIALS

Approx. 20 inches by 11 inches white terry cloth fabric

Scrap of black terry cloth fabric (for eyes*, arms, and ears)

Approx. 20 inches by 11 inches lining fabric

Embroidery floss: black

Embroidery needle

Coordinating thread

Hand-sewing needle

Walking foot if your terry cloth is extra thick (optional)

*Sometimes small pieces of terry cloth may be difficult to hand-sew, so you may want to use black wool felt for the eye pieces instead.

RECOMMENDED FABRICS

Cotton terry or French terry for outer fabric, gauze or muslin for lining fabric

FINISHED DIMENSIONS

7½ inches wide by 7 inches high

CONSTRUCTION STEPS

1 Trace the templates for the panda body, lining, eyes, ears, and arms onto the appropriate fabrics and cut out all the pieces.

method 1:
cut 2 on fold for outer
cut 2 on fold for lining

OR

method 2:
flip over template to trace other half and cut 2 for outer and 2 for lining

cut out of black terry cloth

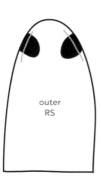

2 Make the ears. Sew the two sets of ears right sides together with a ¼-inch seam allowance. Turn right side out, press, and baste onto the right side of one of the outer pieces.

outer
RS

3 Make the arms. With right sides together, baste the arms to the front and back outer pieces with a ¼-inch seam allowance.

STEP 3

RS

front

RS

back

4 Attach the eye pieces. Hand-stitch the black eye pieces to the outer piece with the basted ears.

5 Add embroidery. Referring to the template or illustration below for placement of facial elements, embroider the eyes and nose using a satin stitch.

6 Sew the outer puppet pieces right sides together with a ¼-inch seam allowance. Trim the seam allowance to about ⅛ inch, turn right side out, and press.

outer
WS

trim seam allowance
to about ⅛"

7 Sew the lining pieces right sides together with a ¼-inch seam allowance, leaving an opening of 2 to 3 inches on one side. Trim the seam allowance to about ⅛ inch except at the opening, turn right side out, and press.

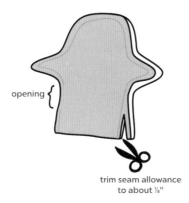

opening {

trim seam allowance
to about ⅛"

8 Assemble the puppet and lining. With the lining wrong side out, place the outer piece, right side out, inside of the lining. Match the raw edges and stitch with a ¼-inch seam allowance around the bottom. It's easier to position the puppet with the presser foot on the inside of the puppet (in this case, the wrong side of the outer piece) than trying to sew from the wrong side of the lining. Turn right side out from the opening left in the lining, slip-stitch the opening closed, push the lining inside of the puppet, and press. Topstitch about ¼ inch from the edge along the bottom.

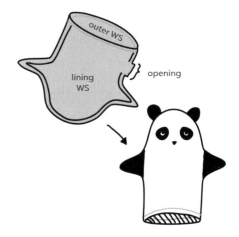

outer WS

lining
WS

opening

Cat

PATTERN PIECES

Cat body (cut 2 from outer fabric, cut 2 from lining fabric)—template (see page 194)

Ears (cut 4)—template (see page 194)

SUPPLIES + MATERIALS

Approx. 20 inches by 11 inches gray terry cloth fabric

Approx. 20 inches by 11 inches lining fabric

Embroidery floss: black, pink, and white

Embroidery needle

Coordinating thread

Hand-sewing needle

Walking foot if your terry cloth is extra thick (optional)

ııııııııııııııııııııııııııııııııııı

RECOMMENDED FABRICS

Cotton terry or French terry for outer fabric, gauze or muslin for lining fabric

ııııııııııııııııııııııııııııııııııı

FINISHED DIMENSIONS

7½ inches wide by 7 inches high

CONSTRUCTION STEPS

1. Trace the templates for the cat body (outer and lining) and ears onto the fabrics and cut out all the pieces.

method 1:
cut 2 on fold for outer
cut 2 on fold for lining

OR

method 2:
flip over template to trace other half and cut 2 for outer and 2 for lining

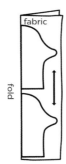

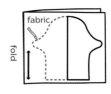

cut 4 ears

2 Make the ears. Sew the two sets of ears right sides together with a ¼-inch seam allowance. Clip the corners. Turn right side out, press, and baste onto the right side of one of the outer pieces.

3 Add embroidery. Referring to the illustration below for placement of facial elements, embroider the eyes, nose, and whiskers using a backstitch for the whiskers and a satin stitch for the eyes and nose.

4 Sew the outer puppet pieces right sides together with ¼-inch seam allowance. Trim the seam allowance to about ⅛ inch, turn right side out, and press.

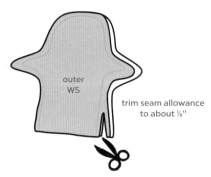

5 Sew the lining pieces right sides together with a ¼-inch seam allowance, leaving an opening of 2 to 3 inches on one side. Trim the seam allowance to about ⅛ inch except at the opening, turn right side out, and press.

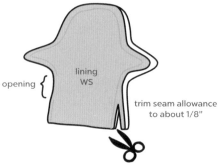

6 Assemble puppet and lining. With lining wrong side out, place the outer piece, right side out, inside of the lining. Match the raw edges and stitch with a ¼-inch seam allowance around the bottom. It's easier to position the puppet with the presser foot on the inside of the puppet (in this case, the wrong side of the outer piece) than trying to sew from the wrong side of the lining. Turn right side out from the opening left in the lining, slip-stitch the opening closed, push the lining inside of the puppet, and press. Topstitch about ¼ inch from the edge along the bottom.

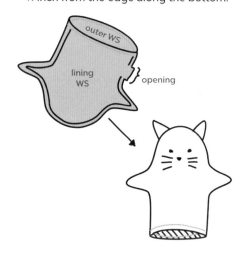

Penguin

PATTERN PIECES

Penguin body (cut 2 from outer fabric, cut 2 from lining fabric)—template (see page 194)

White section for face and stomach (cut 1)—template (see page 194)

SUPPLIES + MATERIALS

Approx. 20 inches by 11 inches black terry cloth fabric

Scrap of white terry cloth fabric

Approx. 20 inches by 11 inches lining fabric

Embroidery floss: black and orange

Embroidery needle

Coordinating thread

Hand-sewing needle

Walking foot if your terry cloth is extra thick (optional)

||||||||||||||||||||||||||||||||||||||||

RECOMMENDED FABRICS

Cotton terry or French terry for outer fabric, gauze or muslin for lining fabric

||||||||||||||||||||||||||||||||||||||||

FINISHED DIMENSIONS

7½ inches wide by 7 inches high

CONSTRUCTION STEPS

1 Trace the templates for the penguin body (outer and lining) and face/stomach onto the appropriate fabrics and cut out all the pieces.

method 1:
cut 2 on fold for outer
cut 2 on fold for lining

OR

method 2:
flip over template to trace other half and cut 2 for outer and 2 for lining

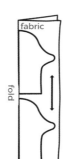

cut stomach piece on fold

2 Attach the face/stomach. Pin and satin/zigzag-stitch white face/stomach piece on the right side of one of the outer pieces.

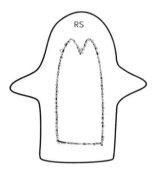

RS

3 Add embroidery. Referring to the illustration below for placement of facial elements, embroider the eyes and beak on the right side of the outer piece from step 2 using a satin stitch.

4 Sew the outer puppet pieces right sides together with a ¼-inch seam allowance. Trim the seam allowance to about ⅛ inch, turn right side out, and press.

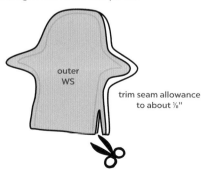

outer
WS

trim seam allowance
to about ⅛"

5 Sew the lining pieces right sides together with a ¼-inch seam allowance, leaving an opening of 2 to 3 inches on one side. Trim the seam allowance to about ⅛ inch except at the opening, turn right side out, and press.

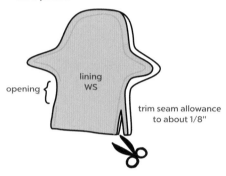

opening {

lining
WS

trim seam allowance
to about 1/8"

6 Assemble puppet and lining. With the lining wrong side out, place the outer piece, right side out, inside of the lining. Match the raw edges and stitch with a ¼-inch seam allowance around the bottom. It's easier to position the puppet with the presser foot on the inside of the puppet (in this case, the wrong side of the outer piece) than trying to sew from the wrong side of the lining. Turn right side out from the opening left in the lining, slip-stitch the opening closed, push the lining inside of the puppet, and press. Topstitch about ¼ inch from the edge along the bottom.

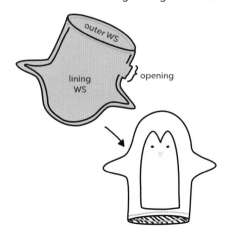

outer WS

lining
WS

} opening

Seal

PATTERN PIECES

Seal body (cut 2 from outer fabric, cut 2 from lining fabric)—template (see page 194)

SUPPLIES + MATERIALS

Approx. 20 inches by 11 inches gray terry cloth fabric

Approx. 20 inches by 11 inches lining fabric (I used gauze)

Embroidery floss: black

Embroidery needle

Coordinating thread

Hand-sewing needle

Walking foot if your terry cloth is extra thick (optional)

RECOMMENDED FABRICS

Cotton terry or French terry for outer fabric, gauze or muslin for lining fabric

FINISHED DIMENSIONS

7½ inches wide by 7 inches high

CONSTRUCTION STEPS

1 Trace the template onto the fabrics and cut out all the pieces.

method 1:
cut 2 on fold for outer
cut 2 on fold for lining

OR

method 2:
flip over template to trace other half and cut 2 for outer and 2 for lining

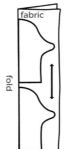

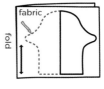

2 Add embroidery. Referring to the illustration below for placement of facial elements, embroider the face on the right side of one of the outer pieces using a satin stitch for the eyes and nose, French knots for the dots, and a backstitch for the whiskers.

3 Sew the outer puppet pieces right sides together with a ¼-inch seam allowance, leaving the bottom open. Trim the seam allowance to about ⅛ inch, turn right side out, and press.

outer
WS

trim seam allowance
to about ⅛"

4 Sew the lining pieces right sides together with a ¼-inch seam allowance, leaving an opening of 2 to 3 inches on one side. Trim the seam allowance to about ⅛ inch except at the opening, turn right side out, and press.

STEP 4

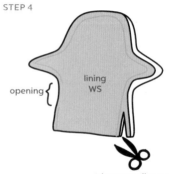

lining
WS

opening {

trim seam allowance
to about 1/8"

5 Assemble the puppet and lining. With the lining wrong side out, place the outer piece, right side out, inside of the lining. Match the raw edges and stitch with a ¼-inch seam allowance around the bottom. It's easier to position the puppet with the presser foot on the inside of the puppet (in this case, the wrong side of the outer piece) than trying to sew from the wrong side of the lining. Turn right side out from the opening left in the lining, slip-stitch the opening closed, push the lining inside of the puppet, and press. Topstitch about ¼ inch from the edge along the bottom.

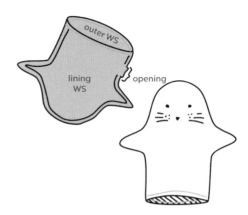

outer WS

lining
WS

opening

Quiet Adventures Felt Book

I MADE A VERSION OF this toy when my daughter was a wee toddler. She loved rearranging shapes and characters that I cut out for her on a big piece of felt. This one is bound like a book for on-the-go entertainment, and a roomy front pocket holds all the loose felt pieces. Templates are included for the felt pieces, and whether you want to keep them simple or add more details is up to you.

PATTERN PIECES

31 inches by 10 inches outer cover (cut
   1 outer, cut 1 lining)—draft

Assorted animals and nature
   elements—templates (see
   pages 195–198)

SUPPLIES + MATERIALS

⅓ yard outer fabric for book cover

⅓ yard lining fabric

5 felt sheets for pages, 9 inches by
   12 inches each (white, black, blue,
   green, gray)

Assorted scraps of felt in various colors
   for animals and nature elements

10 inches of ½-inch-wide elastic or three
   ½-inch buttons

Embroidery floss: colors to match felt
   used (optional)

Embroidery needle (optional)

Hand-sewing needle

Coordinating thread

Drafting kit (see page 41)

Buttonhole foot (if using buttons)

ᴵᴵᴵᴵᴵᴵᴵᴵᴵᴵᴵᴵᴵᴵᴵᴵᴵᴵᴵᴵᴵᴵᴵᴵᴵᴵᴵᴵᴵᴵᴵᴵᴵᴵᴵᴵᴵᴵ

RECOMMENDED FABRICS

For book cover: denim, canvas,
decor-weight fabrics, linen

For lining: cotton, linen, or linen blends

For pages and elements: wool or any
craft felt (felt with wool content usually
sticks together better, though I've used
all kinds of felt successfully)

ᴵᴵᴵᴵᴵᴵᴵᴵᴵᴵᴵᴵᴵᴵᴵᴵᴵᴵᴵᴵᴵᴵᴵᴵᴵᴵᴵᴵᴵᴵᴵᴵᴵᴵᴵᴵᴵ

FINISHED DIMENSIONS

13 inches wide by 9½ inches high
(closed), 28½ inches wide by 9½ inches
high (open)

CONSTRUCTION STEPS

1 Measure and mark the outer cover and lining onto the fabrics and cut them out.

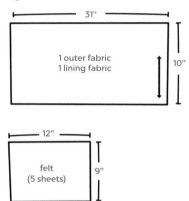

2 Prepare the book cover and lining. Finish the long raw edges of both the outer and lining cover pieces with a zigzag stitch or use a serger/overlocker.

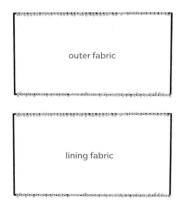

3 Add elastic. If using elastic as the closure, baste the elastic to the top and bottom of the right side of the outer fabric about 3½ inches from the right edge (this will become the front cover). Skip this step if using buttons. Consider not using a closure at all if you want to be extra safe, especially if making this for a baby.

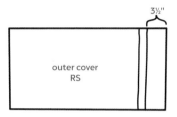

4 Attach the lining. With right sides together, sew the outer piece and lining together with a ½-inch seam allowance on three sides. Leave one of the shorter sides open, which is the side without the elastic. Clip the corners, turn right side out, and press. To create sharp creases, press the seam allowance open first, then press along the folded edges from the right side.

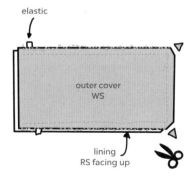

5 Finish the cover edge. Fold the edges of the open end by ¼ inch and press. Fold another ⅜ inch, press, and edgestitch.

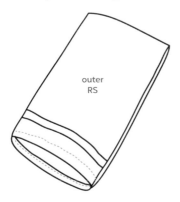

6 Sew the pages into the book. If necessary, trim the felt pages so that they are all even. Place the book cover with the lining facing up. Make sure the closed end is on the right side and the open end is on the left, then align the felt pages to the left edge (open end). Fold over to sandwich the pages, then sew ⅝ inch from the newly folded edge to secure the pages. There will be about 6 inches of the book cover extending from the right edge of the felt pages.

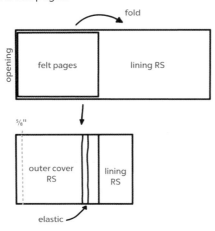

7 Add the closure. For button and buttonholes placement, use the illustration below.

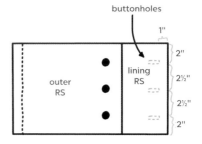

8 Cut out the animals and nature elements from felt. Use the templates to trace the animals and other elements, or come up with your own—the possibilities are endless!

Beanbags

BEANBAG TOSS IS A CLASSIC, nostalgic game. These bags are filled with nontoxic pellets, though beans are obviously a fine option as a filler. And if you opt to skip the decorative embroidery, they can be sewn up in mere minutes. You could also fill them with cotton batting to make them into snuggly softies (or gentler beanbags).

Turtle

PATTERN PIECES

Turtle (cut 2)—template (see page 201)

SUPPLIES + MATERIALS

Approx. ¼ yard green fabric

Embroidery floss: green

Embroidery needle

Coordinating thread

Hand-sewing needle

Beans (pinto or navy) or plastic polypropylene pellets (available online)

Funnel

RECOMMENDED FABRICS

Linen, cotton/linen blend, cotton

FINISHED DIMENSIONS

7 inches wide by 4 inches high

CONSTRUCTION STEPS

1 Trace the template onto the fabric and cut out the pieces.

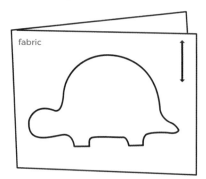

2 Embroider the eyes and shell pattern. Referring to the illustration below for placement of elements, use a satin stitch for the eyes and a running stitch for the turtle shell design.

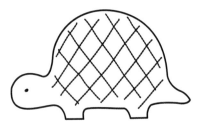

3 Assemble the beanbag. Sew the pieces right sides together with a ¼-inch seam allowance, leaving an opening of 2 to 3 inches at the bottom between the feet. Clip the corners and curves without cutting into the seam. Turn right side out, poking out all the parts, and press.

STEP 3

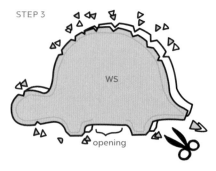

4 Fill the beanbag. Insert a small funnel or rolled-up piece of paper into the opening and fill with beans or plastic pellets (I used about a cup of plastic pellets). Slip-stitch the opening closed. Make sure to securely close the opening to avoid accidental leakage.

Hedgehog

PATTERN PIECES

Hedgehog (cut 2)—template
(see page 200)

SUPPLIES + MATERIALS

Approx. ¼ yard light brown fabric

Embroidery floss: brown

Embroidery needle

Coordinating thread

Hand-sewing needle

Beans (pinto or navy) or plastic
polypropylene pellets
(available online)

Funnel

RECOMMENDED FABRICS

Linen, cotton/linen blend, cotton

FINISHED DIMENSIONS

7½ inches wide by 4½ inches high

CONSTRUCTION STEPS

1 Trace the template onto the fabric and
cut out the pieces.

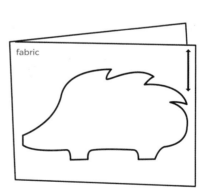

2 Embroider the eyes, nose, and needles. Referring to the illustration below for placement of elements, use a satin stitch for the eyes and nose, and a running stitch for the needles.

3 Assemble the beanbag. Sew the pieces right sides together with a ¼-inch seam allowance, leaving an opening of 2 to 3 inches at the bottom between the feet. Clip the corners and curves without cutting into the seam. Turn right side out, poking out all the parts, and press.

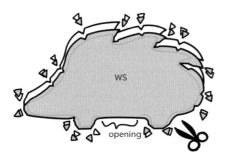

WS

opening

4 Fill the beanbag. Insert a small funnel or rolled-up piece of paper into the opening and fill with beans or plastic pellets (I used about a cup of plastic pellets). Slip-stitch the opening closed. Make sure to securely close the opening to avoid accidental leakage.

Armadillo

PATTERN PIECES

Armadillo (cut 2)—template (see page 199)

Ears (cut 4)—template (see page 199)

SUPPLIES + MATERIALS

Approx. ¼ yard gray fabric

Embroidery floss: silver

Embroidery needle

Coordinating thread

Hand-sewing needle

Beans (pinto or navy) or plastic polypropylene pellets (available online)

Funnel

RECOMMENDED FABRICS

Linen, cotton/linen blend, cotton

FINISHED DIMENSIONS

7 inches wide by 4 inches high

CONSTRUCTION STEPS

1. Trace the templates onto the fabric and cut out the pieces.

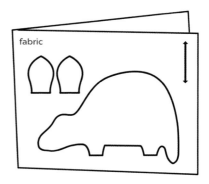

2 Make the ears. Sew the two sets of ears right sides together with a ¼-inch seam allowance. Clip the corners, trim the seam allowance to about ⅛ inch, turn right side out, and press. Slightly overlap the ears and baste onto the right side of the head of one of the armadillo pieces.

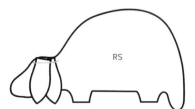

3 Embroider the eyes and "armor" on one side. Referring to the illustration below for placement of elements, use a satin stitch for the eyes and a running stitch for the armor.

4 Assemble the beanbag. With right sides together, sew the pieces with a ¼-inch seam allowance, sandwiching the ears and leaving an opening of 2 to 3 inches at the bottom between the feet. Make sure to move the ears so they don't get accidentally sewn into the bottom part of the armadillo. Clip the corners and curves without cutting into the seam. Turn right side out, poking out all the parts, and press.

STEP 4

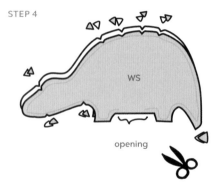

5 Fill the beanbag. Insert a small funnel or rolled-up piece of paper into the opening and fill with beans or plastic pellets (I used about a cup of plastic pellets). Slip-stitch the opening closed. Make sure to securely close the opening to avoid accidental leakage.

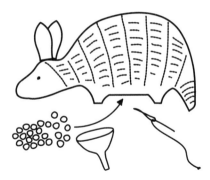

Fishing Game

KIDS AND ADULTS ALIKE GET hooked on this simple yet engaging pastime. Try placing the fish in the Rope Basket (see page 76) or adjust the string length to increase the challenge level. The fish bag will keep everything neatly stored until the next game. This project is an excellent scrap buster, too. Two types of fish templates are included, and the more fish you sew, the more fun the game!

PATTERN PIECES

Bag (cut 2 from outer fabric, cut 2 from lining fabric)—draft

Bag tail (cut 2 from outer fabric)—template (see page 202)

Fish (cut 2)—template (see pages 203 and 204)

SUPPLIES + MATERIALS

¼ yard outer fabric for bag

¼ yard lining fabric for bag

Approx. 13 inches by 9 inches fabric per fish

Coordinating thread

Stuffing (cotton, wool, or fiberfill)

Metal washers (one 1-inch washer per fish)

Magnet*

2 yards twine or cord

Chopstick or small wooden stick

Drafting kit (see page 41)

Hand-sewing needle

Fabric paint or watercolor (optional)

Superglue or hot-glue gun (optional)

Safety pin or bodkin

*Select a size that will not be a choking hazard (the ones used for this project are available online and come with a hook for easy attachment

RECOMMENDED FABRICS

Linen, cotton/linen blend, cotton

FINISHED DIMENSIONS

Fish 1: 7 ½ inches wide by 4 inches high

Fish 2: 7 inches wide by 2 inches high

Bag: 17 ½ inches wide by 8 inches high

CONSTRUCTION STEPS

1 Make the patterns and cut the fabric. Start by drafting the bag piece. Fold a piece of 13-by-9-inch paper in half along the longer edge. Mark 7 inches from the top left edge and 2½ inches down from the upper right edge. Draw a curve to connect the two points and cut along the curve. Unfold the paper, and use this as the template for the fish bag.

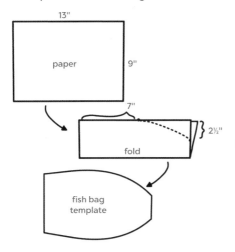

2 Trace all templates onto fabric, and cut out all the pieces.

3 If desired, paint the fabric pieces with fish scales. Make sure to let them dry, then heat-set them with an iron (it's a good idea to use a pressing cloth) before sewing.

4 Make the outer bag. With right sides together, sew one outer bag piece and one tail piece together with a ¼-inch seam allowance. Press the seam toward the tail. Repeat with the other outer bag and tail pieces. With right sides together, sew the two outer bag pieces together with a ⅜-inch seam allowance, starting and ending 1¼ inches from the top edge. Clip the corners and curves.

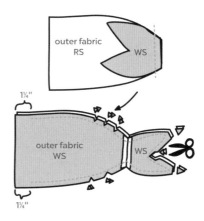

5 Prepare the casing. Zigzag-stitch the unsewn edges at the top. Press the seams open. Fold the zigzag-stitched sections toward the wrong side, press, and edgestitch.

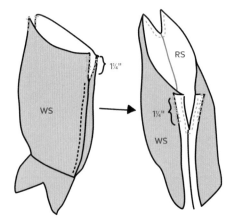

6 Make the bag lining. Repeat the previous steps with the lining pieces, excluding the tail; instead, leave an opening of about 2½ inches along the bottom edge.

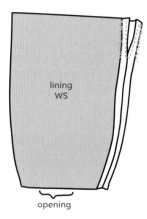

7 Assemble the outer bag and lining. With the outer piece wrong side out, place the lining, right side out, inside of the outer piece and sew together with a ⅜-inch seam allowance along the top edge. Turn right side out from the opening in the lining. Press. To create a casing, topstitch ½ inch from the top edge. Slip-stitch the lining opening closed.

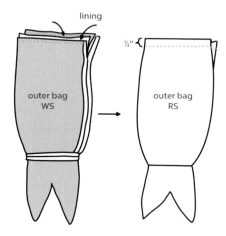

8 Make drawstrings. Using a safety pin or bodkin, thread a 25-inch piece of twine through the casing and tie the ends together. Thread another 25-inch piece of twine the opposite direction and tie the ends together. All done with the bag!

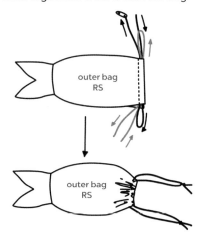

9 Make the fish. Sew the fish pieces right sides together with a ¼-inch seam allowance, leaving an opening of about 2 inches. Clip the corners and curves without cutting into the seam. Turn right side out and press.

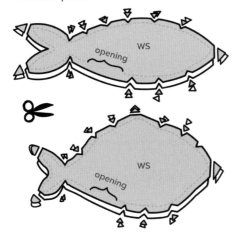

11 Make the fishing rod. Tie a piece of twine on the end of the chopstick, then tie the other end around the magnet. Use super-glue or a hot-glue gun to ensure that the pieces are firmly secured.

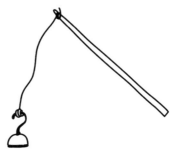

10 Fill the fish lightly with stuffing and place a metal washer inside it. Slip-stitch the opening closed.

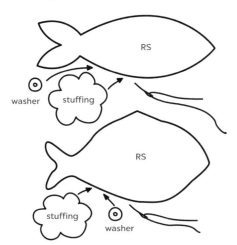

Beanies with Ears

IS THERE ANYTHING CUTER THAN a hat with ears? I think not. Even the grumpiest child can't help but look endearing when sporting a pair of pom-pom or fabric ears. Bonus: these beanies are lightning fast to make, and you'll be able to whip out a dozen before you know it.

PATTERN PIECES

Hat (cut 2 out of outer fabric, cut 2 out of lining fabric)—templates (see pages 205–206)

Ears (cut 4)—template OR make 2 pom-poms (pom-pom maker template included) (see page 205)

ııııııııııııııııııııııııııııııııııı

TIP: Use a zigzag or stretch stitch and a ballpoint or stretch needle for all stretchy fabrics to prevent thread breakage.

SUPPLIES + MATERIALS

Tape

⅓ yard stretchy fabric

⅓ yard stretchy lining fabric

Coordinating thread

Worsted-weight yarn (if making pom-poms)

Hand-sewing needle

POM-POM MATERIALS + SUPPLIES

1 skein yarn

Small piece of cardboard

ııııııııııııııııııııııııııııııııııı

RECOMMENDED FABRICS

Jersey or sweater knit, stretchy Sherpa, or faux fur (sturdier knits with a lot of stretch work great)

ııııııııııııııııııııııııııııııııııı

FINISHED DIMENSIONS

S =   15-inch circumference by 7½ inches high (without ears)— 6 months/baby

M =   16-inch circumference by 8 inches high—12 months/toddler

L =   17-inch circumference by 8½ inches—child/tween

POM-POM CONSTRUCTION STEPS

1 To make the cardboard pom-pom tool, cut a 2½-by-4-inch piece of cardboard. Cut out a slit that is 2½ inches from one edge.

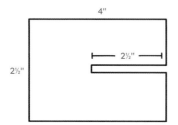

2 Cut a piece of yarn that is about 12 inches long and place it in the slit.

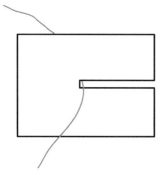

3 Wrap a separate piece of yarn around the cardboard 100 to 120 times, keeping the first piece of yarn out of the way. The more yarn you wrap, the fluffier the pom-pom!

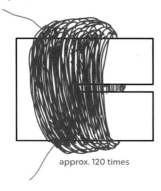

approx. 120 times

4 Tighten the piece of yarn from step 2 around the center of the yarn bundle, wrap twice, and tie as tightly as possible. You may need to slip the yarn bundle off of the cardboard as you do this.

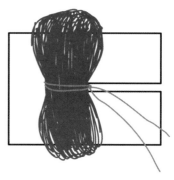

5 Cut the yarn loops at the top and bottom and trim the pom-pom into a circular shape. Make two pom-poms as close in size as possible. Each pom-pom will be about 3 inches in diameter.

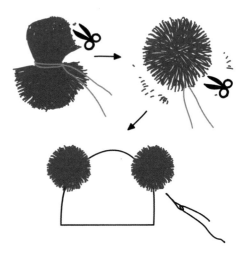

BEANIE CONSTRUCTION STEPS

1. Tape the upper and lower pieces of the beanie template together and cut out the desired size. Trace the template onto the fabric and cut out the outer and lining pieces. Make sure the fabric stretches more side to side when tracing the template and cutting out the fabric pieces.

2. Make the ears. If using pom-poms, skip this step. Sew the ears right sides together with a ¼-inch seam allowance. Remember to use a zigzag stitch for stretchy fabric. Turn right side out and finger-press. Baste the ears to the right side of one of the outer hat pieces where marked, 3 to 4 inches from the pointy tip. Match the marking to the center of the ear.

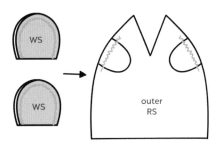

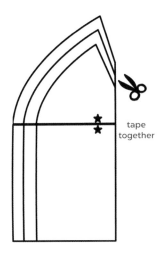

tape together

method 1   method 2

fabric

template WS

fabric

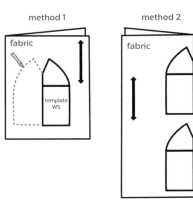

3. Make the beanie (outer hat). With right sides together, pin and sew a short V with a ⅜-inch seam allowance for both outer hat pieces. Then with right sides together and making sure that the short seams from the V line up, pin and sew the two outer pieces together along the curved edge with a ⅜-inch seam allowance.

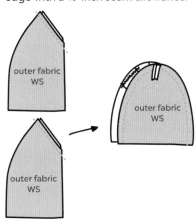

4 Make the lining. Repeat step 3 for the lining pieces, but make sure to leave an opening of about 2 inches on one side of the lining. It's a good idea to sew at least a couple of inches at the bottom of the hat lining before leaving the opening.

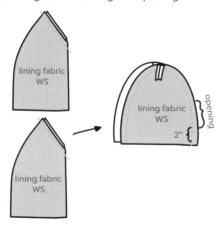

5 Assemble the beanie and lining. With right sides together, sew the hat and lining with a ⅜-inch seam allowance around the bottom edge. The ears will be sandwiched between the two layers. Turn right side out from the lining opening. Slip-stitch the opening closed.

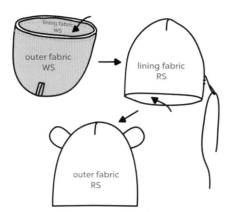

6 Attach the pom-poms. If using pom-poms as ears, follow the instructions on page 126 for how to make them. Hand-sew them on each side of the hat through both layers, securing the thread where the pom-pom is tied at the center. Use the marking on the template as a placement guide.

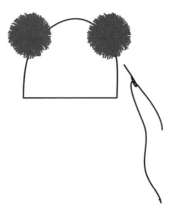

Baby Slippers

KEEP THOSE ITTY-BITTY TOES TOASTY with these soft baby slippers. For maximum comfort, these are designed without any interfacing, though it can be added if you want a little more structure. These have been designed to fit 3-to-6-month-old babies and make an excellent baby gift.

Fox

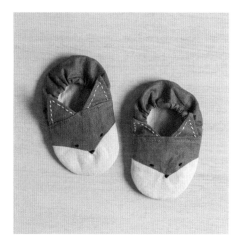

PATTERN PIECES

Heel (cut 2)—template (see page 207)

Fox toe upper section (cut 2)—template (see page 208)

Fox toe lower section (cut 2)—template (see page 208)

Ears (cut 8)—template (see page 208)

Toe lining (cut 2)—template (see page 208)

Sole (cut 2 from outer fabric, cut 2 from lining fabric)—template (see page 207)

SUPPLIES + MATERIALS (PER PAIR)

Approx. ¼ yard red/orange fabric for heel, sole, toe upper section, and ears

Scrap of white fabric for toe lower section

Approx. ¼ yard lining fabric

Coordinating thread

Two 4½-inch-long pieces of ¼-inch-wide elastic

Embroidery floss: black and cream

Embroidery needle

Hand-sewing needle

Safety pin or bodkin

RECOMMENDED FABRICS

Linen, cotton/linen blend, cotton

FINISHED DIMENSIONS

3 inches wide by 5 inches long

CONSTRUCTION STEPS

1 Trace the templates onto the appropriate fabrics and cut out all the pieces.

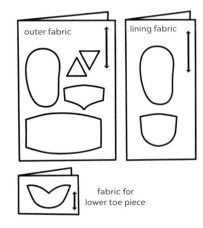

outer fabric

lining fabric

fabric for
lower toe piece

2 Prepare the heel piece. Fold the heel piece in half with wrong sides together and press. Stitch ½ inch from the folded edge. Insert the elastic, and with about ⅜ inch peeking out from one end, stitch in place about ¼ inch from the edge. Then stretch the elastic so that about ⅜ inch is sticking out of the other end, and stitch in place. Trim the excess elastic. Repeat with the other heel piece.

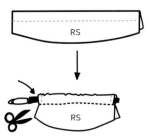

3 Make the toe. With right sides together, pin the upper and lower toe sections from one end to the center, then sew with a ¼-inch seam allowance. Go slow here since the pieces are quite small. Pin the remaining half and sew with a ¼-inch seam allowance. That center bit can be tricky, so don't worry if you can't match up the seams perfectly. You'll be embroidering on top of that section later. Press the seam allowance toward the top.

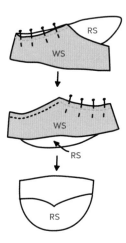

4 To make the ears, sew each set of ears right sides together with a ¼-inch seam allowance. Trim the corners, turn right side out, and press. Topstitch if desired. Fold one of the toe pieces in half to find the center. Pin the ears on either side of the center crease with right sides facing, aligning the raw edges. Baste with a seam allowance just shy of ¼ inch. Repeat with other toe piece and press.

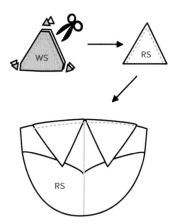

5 Embroider the eyes, ears, and nose. Referring to the illustration below for placement of facial elements, use a satin stitch for the eyes and nose (black floss) and a running stitch for the ears (cream floss).

6 Sew the heel. Attach the heel to the right side of the toe piece by forming a U shape and sewing with a ¼-inch seam allowance. Repeat for the other heel and toe pieces.

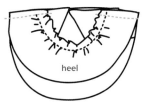

heel

7 Attach the toe lining. Place the toe lining piece on top of the piece from step 6 with the right sides together, sandwiching the heel piece, and stitch across the straight edge with a ¼-inch seam allowance. Trim seam allowance to about ⅛ inch. Flip the toe lining and pull the heel out. Press and topstitch across the top edge. Baste the curved edges together (this makes assembling the slipper easier later).

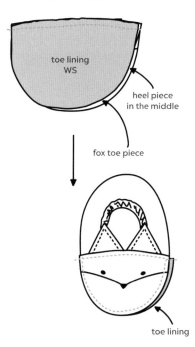

toe lining WS

heel piece in the middle

fox toe piece

toe lining

8 Attach the outer sole. With right sides together, sew the outer sole to the piece from step 7 and baste. Keep in mind that the wider part of the sole aligns with the toe side. Use lots of pins and sew with the top side of the slipper facing up. It might be easier to start by pinning the four sides—the top of the heel, the top of the toe, and the center of each side—then add lots of pins in between.

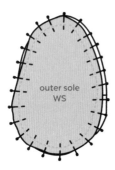

STEP 9

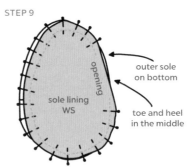

outer sole on bottom

sole lining WS

toe and heel in the middle

opening

side view of layers

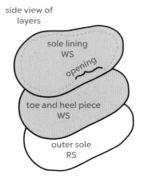

sole lining WS

opening

toe and heel piece WS

outer sole RS

9 Assemble the slipper. Place the right side of the sole lining on top of the wrong side of the toe and heel piece from step 8, sandwiching the slipper between the sole lining and outer sole. Sew around the edge with a ¼-inch seam allowance, leaving an opening of 2 to 3 inches. I like to sew from the outer sole side, following the stitches and adjusting where I might have missed catching all the parts. Trim the seam allowance to about ⅛ inch except for the section with the opening. Turn right side out, adjust the shape, and press. Slip-stitch the opening closed. Repeat with the other slipper, and you're all done!

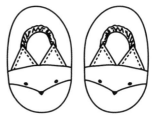

Penguin

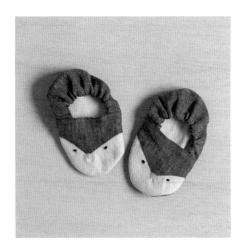

PATTERN PIECES

Heel (cut 2)–template (see page 207)

Penguin toe upper section (cut 2)—
template (see page 208)

Penguin toe lower section (cut 2)—
template (see page 208)

Toe lining (cut 2)—template (see
page 208)

Sole (cut 2 from outer fabric, cut 2
from lining fabric)—template (see
page 207)

SUPPLIES + MATERIALS

Approx. ¼ yard black fabric for heel,
sole, and top of face

Scrap of white fabric for bottom of face

Approx. ¼ yard lining fabric

Coordinating thread

Two 4½-inch-long pieces of ¼-inch-
wide elastic

Embroidery floss: black and yellow

Embroidery needle

Hand-sewing needle

Safety pin or bodkin

||||||||||||||||||||||||||||||||||||||

RECOMMENDED FABRICS

Linen, cotton/linen blend, cotton

||||||||||||||||||||||||||||||||||||||

FINISHED DIMENSIONS

3 inches wide by 5 inches long

CONSTRUCTION STEPS

1 Trace the templates onto the
appropriate fabrics and cut out all
the pieces.

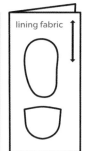

fabric for
lower toe piece

2 Prepare the heel piece. Fold heel piece in half with wrong sides together and press. Stitch ½ inch from folded edge. Insert the elastic, and with about ⅜ inch peeking out from one end, stitch in place about ¼ inch from the edge. Then stretch the elastic so that about ⅜ inch is sticking out of the other end and stitch in place. Trim the excess elastic. Repeat with the other heel piece.

STEP 3

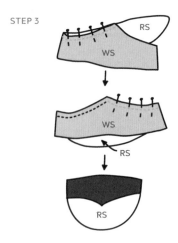

3 Sew the toe. With right sides together, pin the upper and lower toe sections from one end to the center, then sew with a ¼-inch seam allowance. Go slow here since the pieces are quite small. Pin the remaining half and sew with a ¼-inch seam allowance. That center bit can be tricky, so don't worry if you can't match up the seams perfectly. You'll be embroidering on top of that section later. Press the seam allowance toward the top.

4 Embroider the eyes and beak. Referring to the illustration below for placement of facial elements, use a satin stitch.

5 Sew the heel. Attach the heel to the right side of the toe piece by forming a U shape and sewing with a ¼-inch seam allowance. Repeat for the other heel and toe pieces.

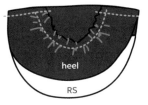

6 Attach the toe lining. Place the toe lining piece on top of the piece from step 5 with the right sides together, sandwiching the heel piece, and stitch across the straight edge with a ¼ inch seam allowance. Trim seam allowance to about ⅛ inch. Flip the toe lining and pull the heel out. Press and topstitch across the top edge. Baste the curved edges together (this makes assembling the slipper easier later).

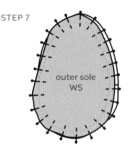

outer sole
WS

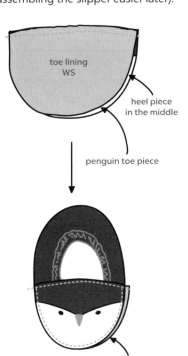

toe lining
WS

heel piece
in the middle

penguin toe piece

toe lining

8 Assemble the slipper. Place the right side of the sole lining on top of the wrong side of the toe and heel piece from step 7, sandwiching the slipper between the sole lining and outer sole. Sew around the edge with a ¼-inch seam allowance, leaving an opening of 2 to 3 inches. I like to sew from the outer sole side, following the stitches and adjusting where I might have missed catching all the parts. Trim the seam allowance to about ⅛ inch except for the section with the opening. Turn right side out, adjust the shape, and press. Slip-stitch opening closed. Repeat with the other slipper, and you're all done!

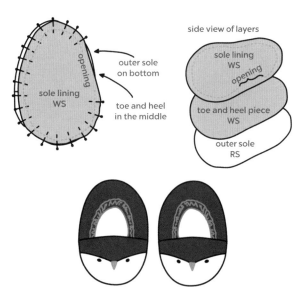

side view of layers

sole lining
WS
opening

toe and heel piece
WS

outer sole
RS

outer sole
on bottom

sole lining
WS

toe and heel
in the middle

opening

7 Attach the outer sole. With right sides together, sew the outer sole to the piece from step 6 and baste. Keep in mind that the wider part of the sole aligns with the toe side. Use lots of pins and sew with the top side of the slipper facing up. It might be easier to start by pinning the four sides—the top of the heel, the top of the toe, and the center of each side—then add lots of pins in between.

Raccoon

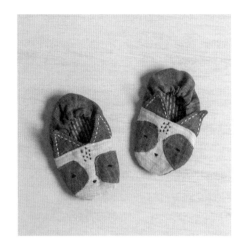

SUPPLIES + MATERIALS

Approx. ¼ yard black fabric for eye patches, ears, heel, and sole

Scrap of white fabric for toes

Approx. ¼ yard lining fabric

Coordinating thread

Two 4½-inch-long pieces of ¼-inch-wide elastic

Embroidery floss: black and white

Embroidery needle

Hand-sewing needle

Safety pin or bodkin

RECOMMENDED FABRICS

Linen, cotton/linen blend, cotton

FINISHED DIMENSIONS

3 inches wide by 5 inches long

PATTERN PIECES

Heel (cut 2)—template (see page 207)

Raccoon toe (cut 2)—template (see page 208)

Raccoon eye patches (cut 4)—template (see page 208)

Ears (cut 8)—template (see page 208)

Toe lining (cut 2)—template (see page 208)

Sole (cut 2 from outer fabric, cut 2 from lining fabric)—template (see page 207)

CONSTRUCTION STEPS

1. Trace the templates onto the appropriate fabrics and cut out all the pieces.

fabric for raccoon face piece

2 Prepare the heel piece. Fold the heel piece in half with wrong sides together and press. Stitch ½ inch from the folded edge. Insert the elastic, and with about ⅜ inch peeking out from one end, stitch in place about ¼ inch from the edge. Then stretch the elastic so that about ⅜ inch is sticking out of the other end and stitch in place. Trim the excess elastic. Repeat with the other heel piece.

elastic

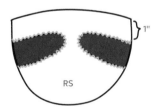

3 Sew the raccoon eye patches. With the right side of the toe piece facing up, pin the eye patches about 1 inch from the top edge on each side (or you may want to hand-baste to avoid the fabric shifting as you appliqué). Appliqué with a satin/zigzag stitch and press. Repeat with the other eye patches and toe piece.

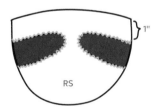

4 To make the ears, sew each set of ears right sides together with a ¼-inch seam allowance. Trim the corners, turn right side out, and press. Topstitch if desired. Fold one of the toe pieces in half to find the center. Pin the ears on either side of the center crease with right sides facing, aligning the raw edges. Baste with a seam allowance just shy of ¼ inch. Repeat with the other toe piece and press.

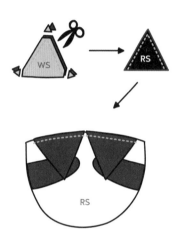

5 Embroider the eyes, nose, and any other decorative elements. Referring to the illustration below for placement of facial elements, use a satin stitch for the eyes and nose and a running stitch for the ears and forehead stitches (keep in mind that the top of the toe piece under the ears will be sewn ¼ inch, so you will want to start your stitches at least ¼ inch from the top). White floss is recommended for the ear details and black floss for the other elements.

STEP 5

6 Sew the heel. Attach the heel to the right side of the toe piece by forming a U shape and sewing with a ¼-inch seam allowance. Repeat for the other heel and toe pieces.

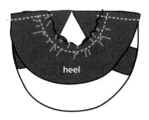

heel

7 Attach the toe lining. Place the toe lining piece on top of the piece from step 6 with right sides together, sandwiching the heel piece, and stitch across the straight edge with a ¼-inch seam allowance. Trim seam allowance to about ⅛". Flip the toe lining and pull the heel out. Press and topstitch across the top edge. Baste the curved edges together (this makes assembling the slipper easier later).

STEP 7

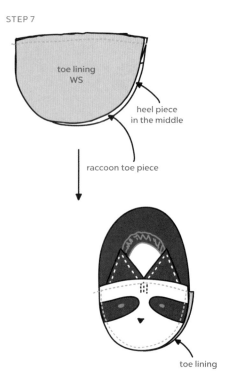

toe lining
WS

heel piece
in the middle

raccoon toe piece

toe lining

8 Attach the outer sole. With right sides together, sew the outer sole to the piece from step 7 and baste. Keep in mind that the wider part of the sole aligns with the toe side. Use lots of pins and sew with the top side of the slipper facing up. It might be easier to start by pinning the four sides—the top of the heel, the top of the toe, and the center of each side—then add lots of pins in between.

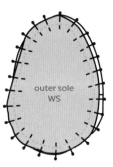

outer sole
WS

9 Assemble the slipper. Place the right side of the sole lining on top of the wrong side of the toe and heel piece from step 8, sandwiching the slipper between the sole lining and outer sole. Sew around the edge with a ¼-inch seam allowance, leaving an opening of 2 to 3 inches. I like to sew from the outer sole side, following the stitches and adjusting where I might have missed catching all the parts. Trim the seam allowance to about ⅛ inch except for the section with the opening. Turn right side out, adjust the shape, and press. Slip-stitch the opening closed. Repeat with the other slipper, and you're all done!

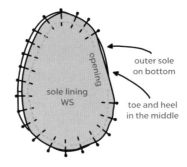

outer sole on bottom

toe and heel in the middle

sole lining WS

opening

side view of layers

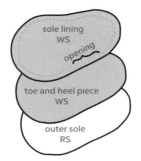

sole lining WS

opening

toe and heel piece WS

outer sole RS

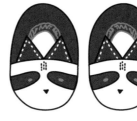

Hooded Capes

SURE TO BE A GO-TO PATTERN when Halloween rolls around, the basic hooded cape is a useful one to have in your arsenal. Here I've rounded up two types of hoods and three types of embellishments that can be mixed and matched to create various animals for dress up. Or you could make a plain hooded cape for unrestricted imaginary play. Alternately, try using terry cloth for a cozy hooded bath towel. There are three sizing options: the small size will fit babies, but please note that infants should not be left unattended with a hooded blanket. The medium size should fit toddlers and preschoolers. The large is meant for elementary/primary school–aged kids.

Animal with Ears

These versatile ears can transform the hooded cape into a mouse or bear or—with a slight folding technique—a horse!

PATTERN PIECES

Hood A (cut 2 from outer fabric, cut 2 from lining fabric)—draft (see page 153)

Front panel (cut 1 from outer fabric, cut 1 from lining fabric)—draft (see page 153)

Cape (cut 1 from outer fabric, cut 1 from lining fabric)—draft (see pages 154–155)

Ears (cut 4; 2 from outer fabric, 2 from lining fabric)—template (see page 209)

SUPPLIES + MATERIALS

2 yards fabric for hood, cape, and ears

2 yards fabric for lining

Coordinating thread

Hand-sewing needle

Two 15-inch-long pieces of ribbon

Drafting kit (see page 41)

Fusible interfacing (optional)

RECOMMENDED FABRICS

Linen, cotton/linen blend, cotton, terry cloth

FINISHED DIMENSIONS

S = Approximately 14 inches wide (neckline) by 9 inches high (hood) by 19½ inches long (cape length) by 34 inches wide (bottom of cape)

M = Approximately 17 inches wide (neckline) by 9½ inches high (hood) by 24 inches long (cape length) by 38 inches wide (bottom of cape)

L = Approximately 20 inches wide (neckline) by 10 inches high (hood) by 29½ inches long (cape length) by 42 inches wide (bottom of cape)

FINISHED DIMENSIONS OF EAR

2½ inches wide by 2½ inches high

CONSTRUCTION STEPS

1. Draft hood A and the cape (see pages 153–155) and cut out the pieces. Trace the templates onto the outer and lining fabrics. To make the front panel piece, you could trace it on the fold with the grainline going up and down (see page 44) or you could trace the half, flip, and trace the other half, then cut out the full front panel piece. The two methods for tracing the front panel are shown below, and the first method is the one used to create the front panel in the layout illustration with the hood and cape template pieces. Cut out all the pieces.

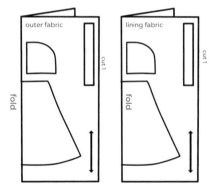

front panel

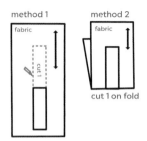

2. Trace the ear template onto the outer and lining fabrics and cut out all the pieces. If you would like the ears to stand up better, iron on fusible interfacing to the wrong side of one of the pieces for each ear.

3. Assemble the outer hood pieces. Sew the outer hood pieces right sides together with a ½-inch seam allowance. Clip the curves without cutting into the seam and press the seam open.

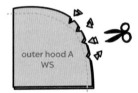

4. To make the ears, sew each set of ear pieces right sides together with a ¼-inch seam allowance. Trim the seam allowance to about ⅛ inch. Turn right side out and press. Align the raw edges, then baste the center of the ears about 3 inches from each side of the outer hood vertical seam. For thinner ears, fold the outer edges toward the center and baste with the folded side facing down.

5 Attach the front panel. With right sides together, pin the front panel to the outer hood front edge and sew with a ½-inch seam allowance. Clip the curves without cutting into the seam, and press the seam allowance open.

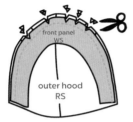

6 Make the hood lining. With right sides together, sew the hood lining pieces with a ½-inch seam allowance. Clip the curves without cutting into the seam and press. Pin the front panel lining to the front edge of the hood lining with right sides together, then sew with a ½-inch seam allowance. Press the seam allowance open.

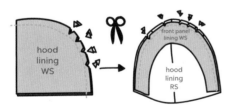

7 Assemble the outer hooded cape. Sew the outer hood and outer cape right sides together at the neckline with a ⅜-inch seam allowance. Press the seam allowance toward the cape.

8 Attach the ribbon. Baste a 15-inch piece of ribbon on both sides of the outer hooded cape, about 1 inch below where the hood meets the cape.

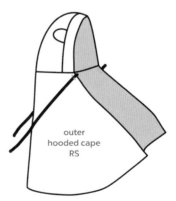

9 Assemble the hooded cape lining. Sew the hood and cape linings right sides together at the neckline with a ⅜-inch seam allowance. Press the seam allowance toward the cape.

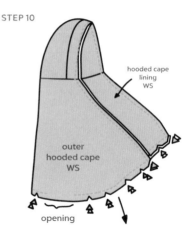

10 Bring it all together: With right sides together, sew the outer hooded cape and lining with a ⅜-inch seam allowance, leaving an opening of about 3 inches in the bottom hem. Arrange the ribbon pieces out of the way between the layers so they don't get accidentally sewn into a seam. Clip the corners and curves, making sure not to cut into the seam. Turn right side out, poking out all sections, and press. Topstitch all around and give it a nice, good press.

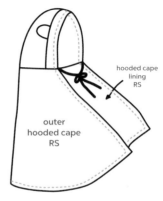

Animal with Horn

A horn is easy and fun to construct and instantly elevates a plain cape to the unicorn of the sea. (Fun fact: a narwhal's horn is actually a tooth!)

PATTERN PIECES

Hood A (cut 2 from outer fabric, cut 2 from lining fabric)—draft (see page 153)

Front panel (cut 1 from outer fabric, cut 1 from lining fabric)—draft (see page 153)

Cape (cut 1 from outer fabric, cut 1 from lining fabric)—draft (see pages 154–155)

Horn (cut 1)—template (see page 210)

SUPPLIES + MATERIALS

2 yards fabric for hood and cape

2 yards fabric for lining and horn

Coordinating thread

Hand-sewing needle

Two 15-inch-long pieces of ribbon

Drafting kit (see page 41)

Fusible interfacing (optional)

RECOMMENDED FABRICS

Linen, cotton/linen blend, cotton, terry cloth

FINISHED DIMENSIONS

S = Approximately 14 inches wide (neckline) by 9 inches high (hood) by 19½ inches long (cape length) by 34 inches wide (bottom of cape)

M = Approximately 17 inches wide (neckline) by 9½ inches high (hood) by 24 inches long (cape length) by 38 inches wide (bottom of cape)

L = Approximately 20 inches wide (neckline) by 10 inches high (hood) by 29½ inches long (cape length) by 42 inches wide (bottom of cape)

FINISHED DIMENSIONS OF HORN

Approximately 7 inches high by 4-inch circumference

CONSTRUCTION STEPS

1. Draft hood A and the cape (see pages 153–155) and cut out the pieces. Trace the templates onto the outer and lining fabrics. To make the front panel piece, you could trace it on the fold with the grainline going up and down (see Sewing Basics on page 44) or you could trace the half, flip, and trace the other half, then cut out the full front panel piece. The two methods for tracing the front panel are shown below, and the first method is the one used to create the front panel in the layout illustration with the hood and cape template pieces. Cut out all the pieces.

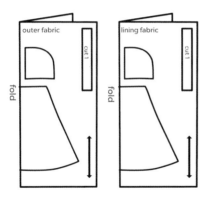

front panel

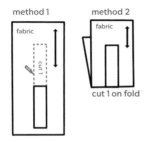

2. Trace the horn template onto the fabric and cut it out.

3. Assemble the outer hood pieces. Sew the outer hood pieces right sides together with a ½-inch seam allowance. Clip the curves without cutting into the seam and press the seam open.

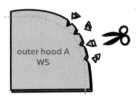

4. Add the front panel. With right sides together, pin the front panel to the outer hood front edge and sew with a ½-inch seam allowance. Clip the curves without cutting into the seam, and press the seam allowance open.

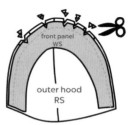

5 To make the horn, sew the long edges of the horn fabric right sides together with a ¼-inch seam allowance. Clip the corner, then turn right side out, poking out the tip (be careful not to poke through!). Fill with stuffing. Thread a needle with heavy-duty thread, and sew with a running stitch along the base of the horn to gather. Next, insert the needle at the base of the horn and start winding the thread tightly around the horn. When you reach the top, insert the needle just beneath the tip of the horn, knot the thread, then insert the needle back through the tip and a couple of inches down. Pull the needle out and clip the thread. You may want to add a touch of fabric glue to keep the thread in place.

6 Make the hood lining. With right sides together, sew the hood lining pieces with a ½-inch seam allowance. Clip the curves without cutting into the seam and press. Pin the front panel lining to the front edge of the hood lining with right sides together, then sew with a ½-inch seam allowance. Press the seam allowance open.

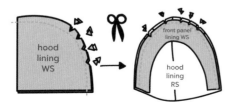

7 Assemble the outer hooded cape. Sew the outer hood and outer cape right sides together at the neckline with a ⅜-inch seam allowance. Press the seam allowance toward the cape.

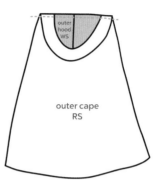

8 Attach the ribbon. Baste a 15-inch piece of ribbon on both sides of the outer hooded cape, about 1 inch below where the hood meets the cape.

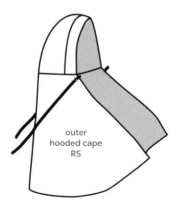

9 Assemble the hooded cape lining. Sew the hood and cape linings right sides together at the neckline with a ⅜-inch seam allowance. Press the seam allowance toward the cape.

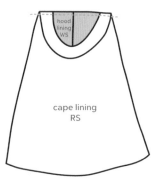

10 Bring it all together: With right sides together, sew the outer hooded cape and lining with a ⅜-inch seam allowance, leaving an opening of about 3 inches in the bottom hem. Arrange the ribbon pieces out of the way between the layers so they don't get accidentally sewn into a seam. Clip the corners and curves, making sure not to cut into the seam. Turn right side out, poking out all sections, and press. Topstitch all around and give it a nice, good press.

STEP 10

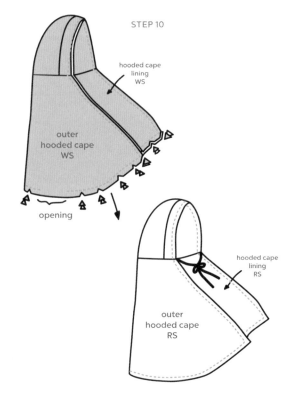

11 Attach the horn. Slip-stitch the horn onto the hood, where the front panel meets the center seam of the hood.

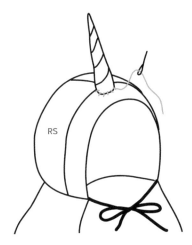

Animal with Bony Plates

Dinosaurs are a perennial staple in the kid world, and this cape is sure to be much beloved year-round.

SUPPLIES + MATERIALS

2 yards fabric for hood and cape

2 yards fabric for lining and bony plates

Coordinating thread

Hand-sewing needle

Two 15-inch-long pieces of ribbon

Drafting kit (see page 41)

Fusible interfacing (optional)

RECOMMENDED FABRICS

Linen, cotton/linen blend, cotton, terry cloth

FINISHED DIMENSIONS

S = Approximately 14 inches wide (neckline) by 9 inches high (hood) by 19½ inches long (cape length) by 34 inches wide (bottom of cape)

M = Approximately 17 inches wide (neckline) by 9½ inches high (hood) by 24 inches long (cape length) by 38 inches wide (bottom of cape)

L = Approximately 20 inches wide (neckline) by 10 inches high (hood) by 29½ inches long (cape length) by 42 inches wide (bottom of cape)

PATTERN PIECES

Hood B (cut 2 from outer fabric, cut 2 from lining fabric)—draft (see page 154)

Cape (cut 2 from outer fabric, cut 2 from lining fabric)—draft (see pages 154–155)

Dino bony plates (cut 10 pairs [small] / 12 pairs [medium] / 14 pairs [large])—template (see page 209)

CONSTRUCTION STEPS

1. Draft hood B and the cape (see pages 154–155) and cut out the pieces. Trace the templates onto the outer and lining fabrics, making sure to add ½ inch to the left edge of the cape for seam allowance. Cut out all the pieces.

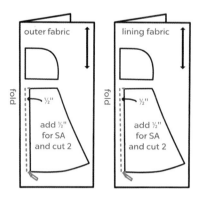

2. Make the bony plates. Using the bony plate template on page 209, trace the appropriate number of triangles onto the fabric and cut out (see Pattern Pieces list on page 149). It's helpful to mark the bottom of the triangles with chalk or by clipping. Iron on fusible interfacing to the wrong side of one (or both, for extra sturdiness) of the triangles of each pair. Sew the triangles right sides together with a ¼-inch seam allowance on two sides, leaving one side open. Clip the corners, turn right side out, and press. Topstitch each triangle if desired. Set aside for now.

STEP 2

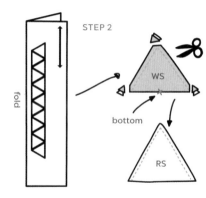

3. Prepare the outer hooded cape for the bony plates. With right sides together, sew one outer hood piece to the corresponding outer cape piece at the neckline with a ⅜-inch seam allowance. Repeat with the other outer hood and cape pieces. Press the seam allowance toward the cape.

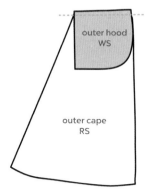

4 Attach the bony plates. Starting ½ inch from the top edge of the hood, align the raw edges and baste the bony plates with right sides together. Continue basting the bony plates along the hooded cape edge, making sure to leave at least ½ inch at the bottom.

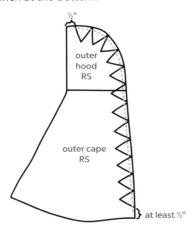

5 Assemble the outer hooded cape. Sew the two outer hooded cape pieces right sides together with a ½-inch seam allowance. Clip the curves without cutting into the seam, press seam open, and flip hooded cape right side out.

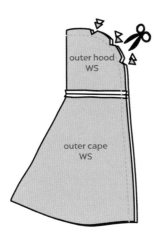

6 Attach the ribbon. Baste a 15-inch piece of ribbon on both sides of the outer hooded cape, about 1 inch below where the hood meets the cape.

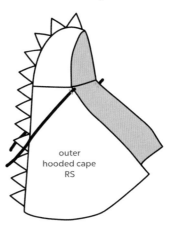

7 Assemble the hood lining and cape lining. With right sides together, sew one hood lining piece to the corresponding cape lining piece at the neckline with a ⅜-inch seam allowance. Repeat with the other hood and cape lining pieces. Press the seam open. With right sides together, sew the hooded cape lining pieces along the outer curve with a ½-inch seam allowance. Press the seam open.

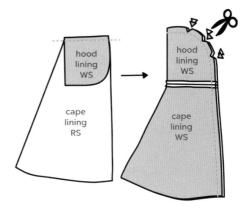

8 Bring it all together: With right sides together, sew the outer hooded cape and lining with a ⅜-inch seam allowance, leaving an opening of about 3 inches in the bottom hem. Arrange the ribbon pieces out of the way between the layers so they don't get accidentally sewn into a seam. Clip the corners and curves, making sure not to cut into the seam. Turn right side out, poking out all sections, and press. Topstitch all around and give it a nice, good press.

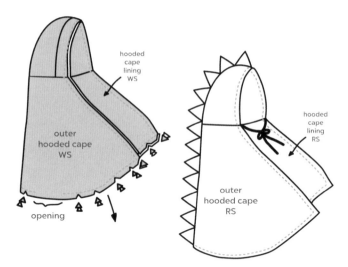

hooded cape lining WS

outer hooded cape WS

opening

hooded cape lining RS

outer hooded cape RS

MIX-AND-MATCH VARIATIONS

Add a horn to the cape with ears to transform it into a unicorn; create a dragon by adding ears to the cape with bony plates! For the ears, fold the outer edges of the ears so they meet in the center and baste before attaching to the hood.

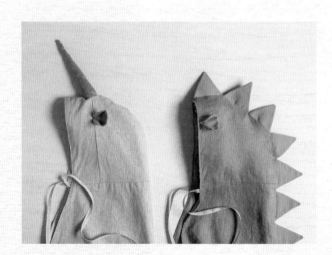

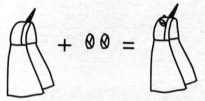

animal with horn + folded ears = unicorn

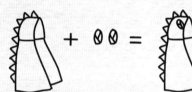

animal with bony plates + folded ears = dragon

Drafting Hood + Cape Templates

HOOD A

This hood has a front panel, which enables the attachment of ears.

1 Draft the hood pattern on a piece of paper that is at least 8 inches wide and 11 inches high. You could also draft directly on the fabric. Using the dimensions provided below for the size you need, start by drawing a rectangle of the appropriate size:

Hood width: small (6½ inches) / medium (7 inches) / large (7½ inches)

Hood height: small (9 inches) / medium (9½ inches) / large (10 inches)

STEP 2

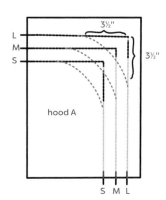

hood A

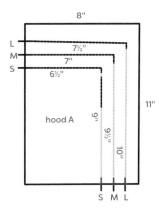

hood A

2 Draw a curve starting about 3 to 3½ inches left of the top right corner and ending about 3 to 3½ inches below the top right corner. You don't need to be too exact here, though it will fit the head better the more rounded it is. Cut out the hood pattern piece.

3 On a piece of paper that is at least 5 inches wide and 10 inches high, create the front panel using the measurements provided below. Cut out the template piece, and mark "fold" on one of the shorter ends. You will be cutting out one piece on the fold from the fabric.

Width: small (3 inches) / medium (3½ inches) / large (4 inches)

Height: small (8½ inches) / medium (9 inches) / large (9½ inches)

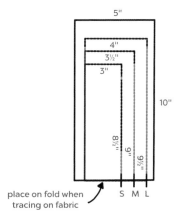

place on fold when
tracing on fabric

HOOD B

This is a simpler hood that is almost exactly like hood A but without the front panel.

1 Draft the hood pattern on a piece of paper that is at least 11 inches high and 11 inches wide. You could also draft directly on the fabric. Using the dimensions provided below for the size you need, start by drawing a rectangle of the appropriate size:

Hood width = small (8 inches) / medium (9 inches) / large (10 inches)

Hood height = small (8½ inches) / medium (9½ inches) / large (10½ inches)

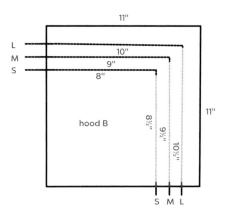

2 Draw a curve starting about 3 to 3½ inches left of the upper right corner and ending about 3 to 3½ inches below the upper right corner. You don't need to be too exact here, though it will fit the head better the more rounded it is. Cut out the hood pattern piece.

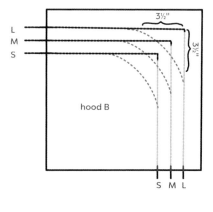

CAPE

1 Take a large piece of paper that is at least 32 inches long and 25 inches wide (you may need to tape some pieces together if you don't have Swedish tracing paper or large paper). Or you could draft directly onto the fabric, though the fabric must be folded on the left edge. Make sure you have a straight edge on the top and left, then mark three points (A, B, and C) from the left edge using the dimensions provided on page 155 in the size you need. A yardstick or very long ruler is helpful for drafting this pattern piece.

SMALL

A = 7½ inches to the right (8 inches for cape with bony plates)

B = 20 inches down from top left edge

C = 18 inches to the right from B

MEDIUM

A = 8½ inches to the right (9 inches for cape with bony plates)

B = 25 inches down from top left edge

C = 20 inches to the right from B

LARGE

A = 9½ inches to the right (10 inches for cape with bony plates)

B = 30 inches down from top left edge

C = 22 inches to the right from B (if the fabric shrinks in the wash, 21 inches works fine too)

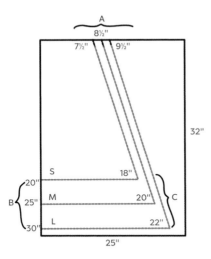

NOTE: The exception is if you are making the cape with the dino bony plates, in which case you will use the measurements listed above but add ½ inch along the left for the seam allowance, and you will *not* be cutting on the fold.

NOTE

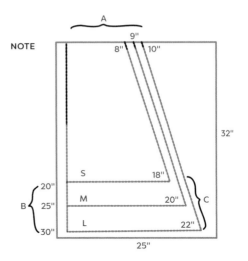

2   Connect points A and C. Curve the bottom of the cape, but retain a right angle where point A and C meet. Don't worry about getting the curve exactly right; it's more important to have a right angle at the corner. As a general guide, the end points of the curves will be less than 2 inches on the vertical line and less than 4 inches on the horizontal line. Mark "fold" on the left edge. Except for the Animal with Bony Plates cape, you will be cutting the cape and cape lining on the fold.

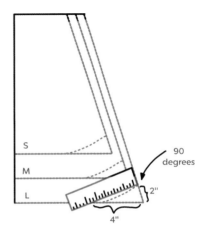

Bibs

THE BANE OF MEALTIMES WITH the high-chair bound is the food flinging and liquid dribbling, as we all know. These sassy animal bibs come with a generous pocket that will catch a good portion of those foods and liquids.

Monkey

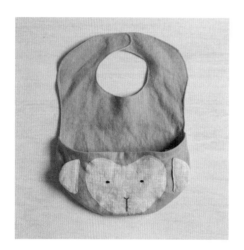

PATTERN PIECES

Bib (cut 1 from outer fabric, cut 1 from lining fabric)—template (see pages 212 and 214)

Ears (4)—template (see page 211)

Face (cut 1)—template (see page 211)

Pocket (cut 2)—template (see page 213)

SUPPLIES + MATERIALS

Tape

⅓ yard beige fabric for bib, pocket, and ears

Scrap of white fabric for face

Coordinating thread

Hand-sewing needle

Embroidery floss: black

Embroidery needle

Velcro closure (1-inch by ¾-inch sticky-back ovals designed for fabric work well) or size 4 sew-on snaps

RECOMMENDED FABRICS

Linen, cotton/linen blend, cotton

FINISHED DIMENSIONS

10 inches wide by 13 inches high

CONSTRUCTION STEPS

1 Trace the template pieces and cut them out. Tape the upper and lower template parts of the bib together. Trace the taped bib template onto the fabric, then flip the template to mirror and trace the other half. I used the same fabric for both the outer and lining pieces. Trace the other templates onto the appropriate fabrics (mirror the pocket template as well), and cut them all out.

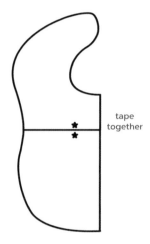

tape together

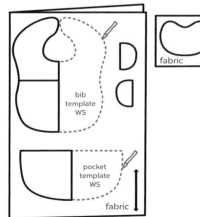

2 To make the face, satin/zigzag-stitch the face to the center of the right side of one of the pocket pieces. I like to fold the pocket piece in half to create a center crease, then do the same with the face piece. Align the center creases.

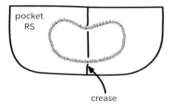

crease

3 Make the ears. Sew the ears right sides together with a ¼-inch seam allowance along the curve. Leave the straight edge open. Trim the seam allowances to about ⅛ inch. Turn right side out and press, tucking in the raw edges about ¼ inch. Sew the ears to the right side of the pocket piece, about ½ inch from each side of the face.

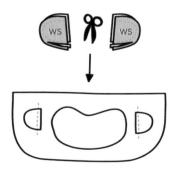

4 Embroider the eyes and nose. Referring to the template or illustration below for placement of facial elements, use a satin stitch for the eyes and a backstitch for the nose.

5 Make the pocket. Sew the pocket pieces right sides together along the top straight edge with a ¼-inch seam allowance. Turn right side out and press. Topstitch and press. Keep in mind that the pocket is bigger than the bib's lower curved edge. This is to create a protruding pouch (the better to catch all the flying food!). Match the raw edges and markings along the right side of one of the bib pieces, pin, and baste the pocket to the bib.

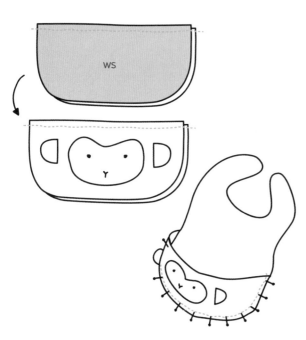

6 Finish the bib. With right sides together, sew the bib pieces with a ⅜-inch seam allowance, leaving an opening of about 3 inches near the top of the bib. Clip the curves of the seam allowance, making sure not to cut into the seam. Turn right side out, push and smooth out the bib edges, and press. Topstitch.

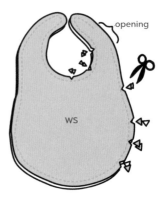

opening

WS

7 Add the closure. Attach sticky-back Velcro onto the bib ends, making sure to attach one Velcro piece on the front side and the other Velcro piece on the underside. Alternatively, use sew-on snaps. All done!

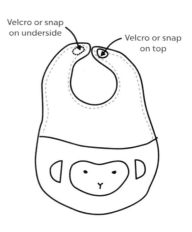

Velcro or snap on underside

Velcro or snap on top

Koala

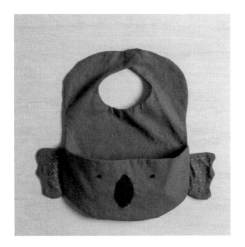

SUPPLIES + MATERIALS

Tape

⅓ yard gray fabric for bib, pocket, and ears

Scrap of black fabric for nose

Coordinating thread

Hand-sewing needle

Embroidery floss: black

Embroidery needle

Velcro closure (1-inch by ¾-inch sticky-back ovals designed for fabric work well) or size 4 sew-on snaps

RECOMMENDED FABRICS

Linen, cotton/linen blend, cotton

FINISHED DIMENSIONS

13 inches wide (with ears) by 13 inches high

PATTERN PIECES

Bib (cut 1 from outer fabric, cut 1 from lining fabric)—template (see pages 212 and 214)

Ears (4)—template (see page 211)

Nose (cut 1)—template (see page 211)

Pocket (cut 2)—template (see page 213)

CONSTRUCTION STEPS

1 Trace the template pieces and cut them out. Tape the upper and lower template parts of the bib together. Trace the taped bib template onto the fabric, then flip the template to mirror and trace the other half. I used the same fabric for both the outer and lining pieces. Trace the other templates onto the appropriate fabrics (mirror the pocket template as well), and cut them all out.

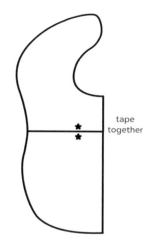

tape together

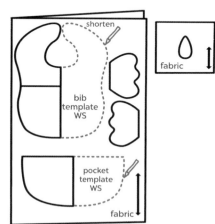

2 Make the ears. Using three or four strands of floss, embroider the front side of the left and right ears with decorative stitches if desired. Sew along the outer edge of the ears, right sides together, with a ¼-inch seam allowance; leave the straighter edge open. Clip the curves, turn right side out, and press. Baste the ears to the right side of one of the pocket pieces where marked, 1 inch from the top edge on each side.

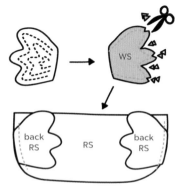

3 Add the nose and embroider the eyes. Fold the pocket piece in half to create a center crease. Satin/zigzag-stitch the nose to the center of the right side of the pocket piece with the basted ears. Referring to the template or illustration below for placement of eyes, embroider with a satin stitch.

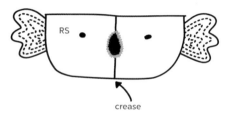

crease

4 Make the pocket. With the ears opened out to avoid sewing into them, sew the pocket pieces right sides together along the top straight edge with a ¼-inch seam allowance. Turn right side out and press. Topstitch and press. Keep in mind that the pocket is bigger than the bib's lower curved edge. This is to create a protruding pouch (the better to catch all the flying food!). Match the raw edges and markings along the right side of one of the bib pieces, pin, and baste the pocket to the bib.

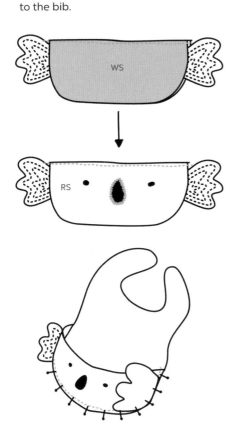

5 Finish the bib. With right sides together, sew the bib pieces with a ⅜-inch seam allowance, leaving an opening of about 3 inches near the top of the bib. Clip the curves of the seam allowance, making sure not to cut into the seam. Turn right side out, push and smooth out the bib edges, and press. Topstitch.

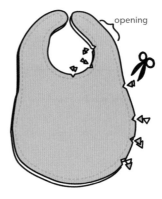

opening

6 Add the closure. Attach sticky-back Velcro onto the bib ends, making sure to attach one Velcro piece on the front side and the other Velcro piece on the underside. Alternatively, use sew-on snaps. All done!

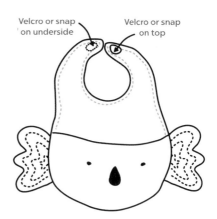

Velcro or snap on underside

Velcro or snap on top

Backpacks

THIS EASY BACKPACK IS PRETTY much guaranteed to be a crowd-pleaser. The deceptively small size will hold a change of clothes, snacks, and maybe even a lovey. The fox version is designed with a front pocket that can be added to the sheep backpack as well, if desired.

Sheep

PATTERN PIECES

Bag (cut 2 from outer fabric, cut 2 from
lining fabric)—draft

Face (cut 2)—template (see page 215)

Ears (cut 4)—template (see page 217)

SUPPLIES + MATERIALS

Approx. ¼ yard black fabric for face
and ears

Approx. ½ yard Sherpa fabric for
outer bag

Approx. ½ yard lining fabric

2 yards 1-inch webbing

Two 1-inch metal slide buckles

Embroidery floss: black

Embroidery needle

2 pieces of ¼-inch-wide ribbon or
cord for drawstring, each about
25 inches long

Coordinating thread

Hand-sewing needle

Size 4 sew-on snaps or size 20
KAM snaps

Drafting kit (see page 41)

RECOMMENDED FABRICS

Linen, cotton/linen blend, cotton,
Sherpa for sheep backpack

FINISHED DIMENSIONS

11 inches wide by 15 inches high
13 inches wide (with ears) by
15 inches high

CONSTRUCTION STEPS

1 Trace the templates for the face and ears onto the black fabric and cut them out. On the Sherpa and lining fabrics, measure out 12 inches by 16 inches for bag and lining pieces and cut them out.

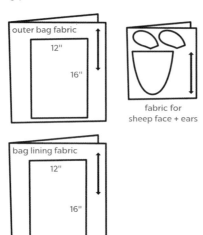

2 Assemble the sheep face. Sew each set of ears right sides together with a ¼-inch seam allowance. Clip the corners and curves without cutting into the seam, turn right side out, and press. Topstitch if desired. Baste ears onto the right side of one of the face pieces at the markings.

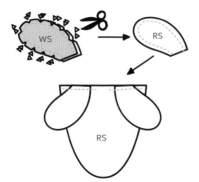

3 Embroider the eyes and nose. Referring to the illustration below for placement of the eyes and nose, use a satin stitch to embroider on the face piece with the basted ears.

4 Sew the face lining. With the ears moved out of the way, sew the face pieces right sides together along the curved edge with a ⅜-inch seam allowance. Leave the top edge open. Clip the corners and curves, making sure not to cut into the seam. Turn right side out and press.

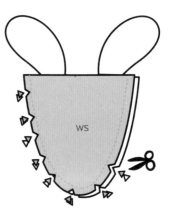

5 Attach the straps. From the webbing, cut two straps to 20 inches in length and two straps to 16 inches in length. With the right side of the back bag piece facing up, angle and overlap the two longer straps at the center of the back bag piece and baste about ¼ inch from the top. Trim the excess webbing. Measure 2 inches from the bottom of each side of the same bag piece, and baste the shorter straps about ¼ inch from each side.

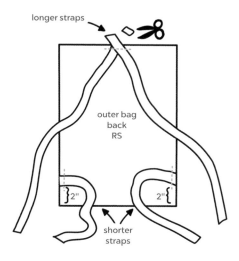

longer straps

outer bag
back
RS

2" 2"

shorter
straps

6 Attach the sheep face to the outer bag. With right sides together and with a seam allowance of about ¼ inch, baste the sheep face to the back of the outer bag, centering the face piece where the longer straps are basted.

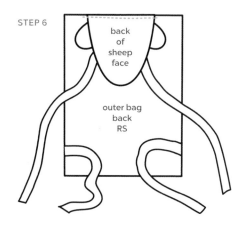

back
of
sheep
face

outer bag
back
RS

7 Sew the outer bag. For Sherpa fabric, serge or zigzag-stitch the raw edges first. Mark 1½ inches from each top corner toward the bottom. With right sides together, sew three sides of the outer bag with a ⅜-inch seam allowance beginning and ending at the 1½-inch marks, sandwiching the side straps and making sure they don't get caught in other parts of the seam. On each side, finish a couple of inches of the raw edges from the top (if you haven't zigzag-stitched or serged it yet), fold and press the seam allowance toward the wrong side, and edgestitch in place.

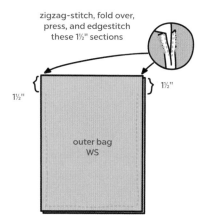

zigzag-stitch, fold over,
press, and edgestitch
these 1½" sections

1½" 1½"

outer bag
WS

8 Box the corners of the outer bag by flattening the left and right bottom corners to form a triangle. The easiest way to form the triangle is to pinch each side of the corner and pull outward. Measure 2 inches from the tip of the triangle and sew diagonally. Trim to ¼ inch.

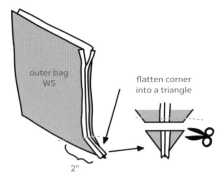

outer bag
WS

flatten corner
into a triangle

2"

9 Sew the lining. Repeat steps 7 and 8, but leave an opening of 3 to 4 inches at the bottom.

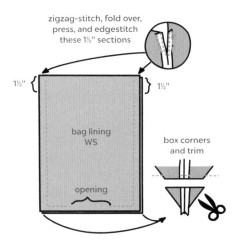

zigzag-stitch, fold over, press, and edgestitch these 1½" sections

1½"   1½"

bag lining
WS

box corners
and trim

opening

10 Assemble the bag and lining. With the wrong side of the lining facing outward, insert the bag, right side out. Sew the bag and lining right sides together with a ⅜-inch seam allowance along the top edge. Turn right side out from the opening in the lining and press. Slip-stitch the opening in the lining closed.

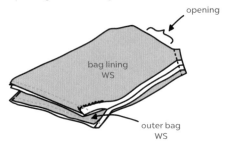

opening

bag lining
WS

outer bag
WS

11 Make the drawstrings. Sew ⅝ inch from the top to create the drawstring casing. Sew under the face and straps on the back side. Thread a 25-inch ribbon or cord from one side using a bodkin or safety pin, and tie the ends together. Then thread another 25-inch ribbon or cord from the opposite direction.

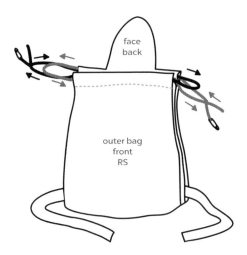

face
back

outer bag
front
RS

12 Finish the straps by adding slide buckles to the longer straps. Wrap the strap around the middle bar, fold the edge under by about 2 inches, and stitch to the underside of the strap (alternatively, zigzag-stitch the edge to prevent fraying, skip the fold, and stitch to the underside of the strap). Thread the side straps into the slide buckle to secure.

13 Add the closure. Sew on snaps or attach KAM snaps. If using snaps, stitch the top snap only to the lining layer of the face. Or, for extra kid-friendliness, forego snaps altogether!

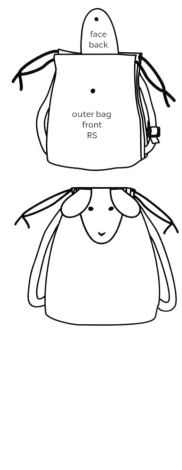

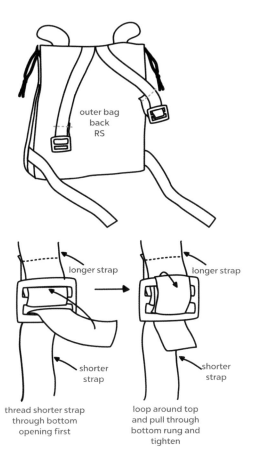

thread shorter strap through bottom opening first

loop around top and pull through bottom rung and tighten

Fox

PATTERN PIECES

Bag (cut 2 from outer fabric, cut 2 from lining fabric)—draft

Face (cut 2)—template (see page 215)

Snout (cut 1)—template (see page 216)

Ears (cut 4)—template (see page 216)

Inner ears (cut 2)—template (see page 216)

Pocket (cut 2)—template (see page 217)

SUPPLIES + MATERIALS

Approx. ½ yard fabric for snout, ears, and outer bag

Approx. ¼ yard white fabric for face, inner ears, and pocket

Approx. ½ yard lining fabric

2 yards 1-inch webbing

Two 1-inch metal slide buckles

Embroidery floss: black

Embroidery needle

2 pieces of ¼-inch ribbon or cord for drawstring, each about 25 inches long

Coordinating thread

Hand-sewing needle

Size 4 sew-on snaps or size 20 KAM snaps

RECOMMENDED FABRICS

Linen, cotton/linen blend, cotton

FINISHED DIMENSIONS

11 inches wide by 15 inches high

CONSTRUCTION STEPS

1 Trace the templates onto the appropriate fabrics and cut them out. On the outer and lining fabrics, measure out 12 inches by 16 inches for the bag and lining pieces and cut them out.

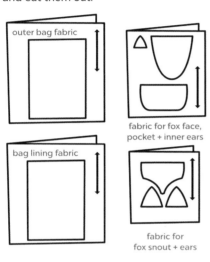

2 Sew the fox snout. Appliqué the snout with a satin/zigzag stitch on the right side of one of the face pieces.

3 Sew the ears. Center and align the bottom of the inner ear with right side facing up and on top of the right side of the outer ear. Pin and appliqué the top two sides with a satin/zigzag stitch. Repeat with the other inner ear and outer ear pieces. Sew each set of ears right sides together with a ¼-inch seam allowance. Clip the corners, trim the seam allowance to about ⅛ inch, turn right side out, and press. Topstitch if desired. Align the raw edges and baste onto the right side of the face piece with the appliquéd snout.

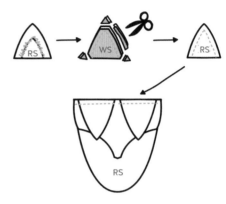

4 Embroider the eyes and nose. Referring to the illustration below for placement of the eyes and nose, use a satin stitch to embroider on the face piece with the basted ears.

5 Sew the face lining. With the ears moved out of the way, sew the face pieces right sides together along the curved edge with a ⅜-inch seam allowance. Leave the top edge open. Clip the corners and curves, making sure not to cut into the seam. Turn right side out and press.

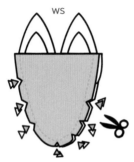

6 Sew the pocket. For a sturdier pocket, iron on fusible interfacing to the wrong side of the lining piece. Sew the pocket pieces right sides together with a ¼-inch seam allowance, leaving an opening of 2 to 3 inches along the straight side at the top. Clip the corners and curves, turn right side out, and press. Topstitch the straight edge closed. Measure and mark 5 inches from the bottom center of one of the outer bag pieces, place the bottom of the pocket at the mark, and center the pocket. Edgestitch the bottom and sides of the pocket onto the bag, leaving the top open. This will be the front of the bag.

STEP 6

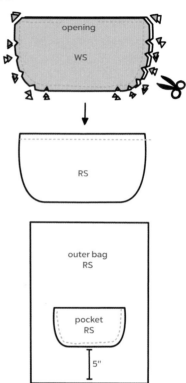

7 Attach the straps. From the webbing, cut two straps to 20 inches in length and two straps to 16 inches in length. With the right side of the back bag piece facing up, angle and overlap the two longer straps at the center of the back bag piece and baste about ¼ inch from the top. Trim the excess webbing. Measure 2 inches from the bottom of each side of the same bag piece and baste the shorter straps about ¼ inch from each side.

STEP 7

longer straps

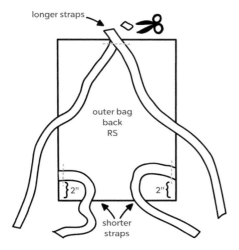

8 Attach the fox face. With right sides together and with a seam allowance of about ¼ inch, baste the fox face to the back of the outer bag, centering the face piece with the ears folded down where the longer straps are basted.

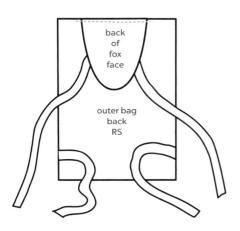

9 Sew the outer bag. Mark 1½ inches from each top corner toward the bottom. With right sides together, sew three sides of the outer bag with a ⅜-inch seam allowance beginning and ending at the 1½-inch marks, sandwiching the side straps and making sure they don't get caught in other parts of the seam. On each side, finish a couple of inches of the raw edges from the top, fold and press the seam allowance toward the wrong side, and edgestitch in place.

zigzag-stitch, fold over, press, and edgestitch these 1½" sections

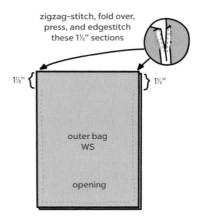

10 Box the corners of the outer bag by flattening the left and right bottom corners to form a triangle. The easiest way to form the triangle is to pinch each side of the corner and pull outward. Measure 2 inches from the tip of the triangle and sew diagonally. Trim to ¼ inch.

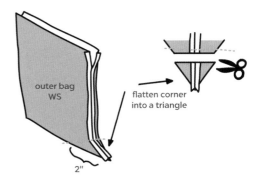

flatten corner into a triangle

11 Sew the lining. Repeat steps 9 and 10, but leave an opening of 3 to 4 inches at the bottom.

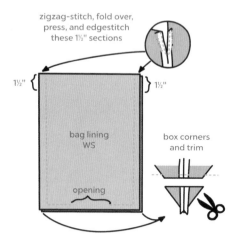

zigzag-stitch, fold over, press, and edgestitch these 1½" sections

1½"

1½"

bag lining
WS

box corners
and trim

opening

12 Assemble the bag and lining. With the wrong side of the lining facing outward, insert the bag, right side out. Sew the bag and lining right sides together with a ⅜-inch seam allowance along the top edge. Turn right side out from the opening in the lining and press. Slip-stitch the opening in the lining closed.

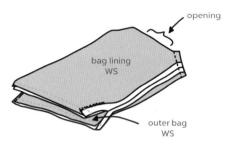

opening

bag lining
WS

outer bag
WS

13 Make the drawstrings. Sew ⅝ inch from the top to create the drawstring casing. Sew under the face and straps on the back side. Thread a 25-inch ribbon or cord from one side using a bodkin or safety pin, and tie the ends together. Then thread another 25-inch ribbon or cord from the opposite direction.

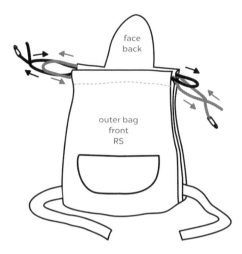

face
back

outer bag
front
RS

14 Finish the straps by adding slide buckles to the longer straps. Wrap the strap around the middle bar, fold the edge under by about 2 inches, and stitch to the underside of the strap (alternatively, zigzag-stitch the edge to prevent fraying, skip the fold, and stitch to the underside of the strap). Thread the side straps into the slide buckle to secure.

STEP 14

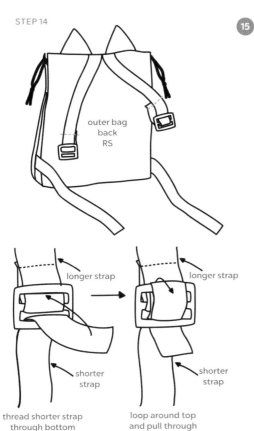

outer bag
back
RS

longer strap

longer strap

shorter
strap

shorter
strap

thread shorter strap
through bottom
opening first

loop around top
and pull through
bottom rung and
tighten

15 Add the closure. Sew on snaps or attach KAM snaps. If using snaps, stitch the top snap only to the lining layer of the face. Or, for extra kid-friendliness, forego snaps altogether!

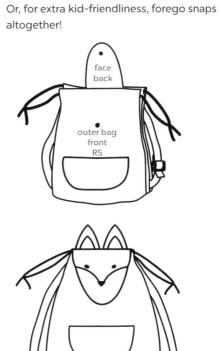

face
back

outer bag
front
RS

Templates

TO PRESERVE THE TEMPLATES, USE TRACING paper (Swedish tracing paper is great for this) to transfer them with pen or pencil. Cut the traced templates out, and place on the fabric for further tracing and cutting.

Templates are typically traced on the wrong side of the fabric unless you want a particular section of a printed fabric on the pattern piece. Seam allowances are included for all templates, and each template indicates the number of pieces that need to be cut. For example, "cut 2" will mean you will cut two mirrored pieces by folding the fabric in half with the right sides together and tracing the template on the wrong side. When you see "Fold" on the template, you can do one of two things: place it on the fabric fold, or trace one half on the fabric, then flip the template to trace the other half.

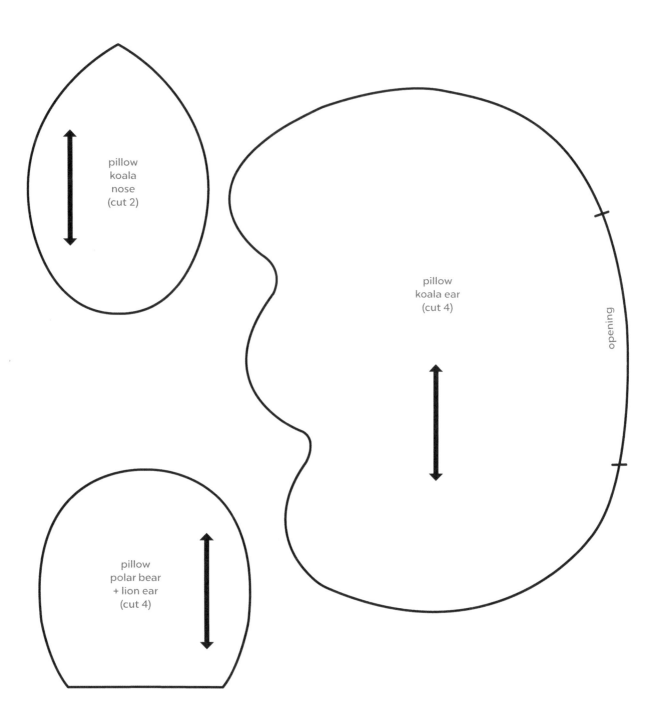

pillow
koala
nose
(cut 2)

pillow
koala ear
(cut 4)

opening

pillow
polar bear
+ lion ear
(cut 4)

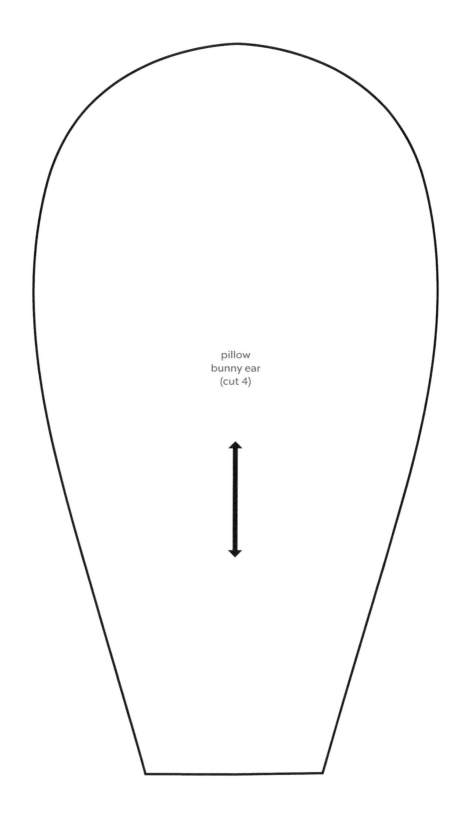

pillow
bunny ear
(cut 4)

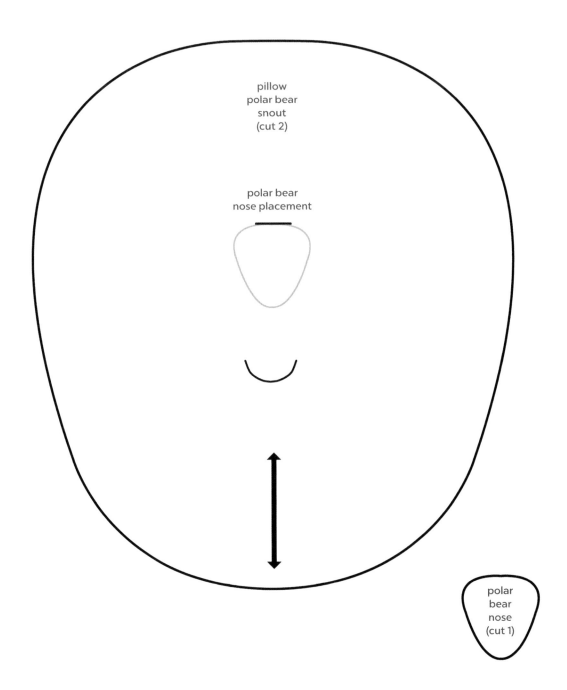

pillow
polar bear
snout
(cut 2)

polar bear
nose placement

polar
bear
nose
(cut 1)

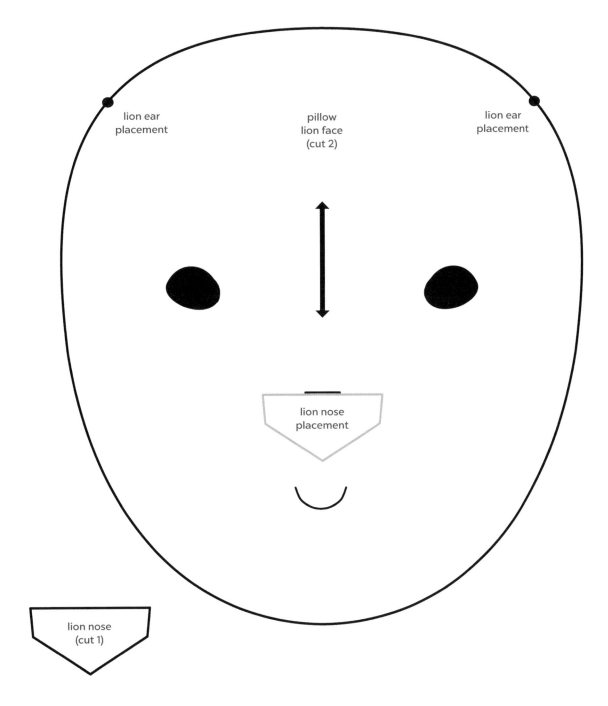

lion ear
placement

pillow
lion face
(cut 2)

lion ear
placement

lion nose
placement

lion nose
(cut 1)

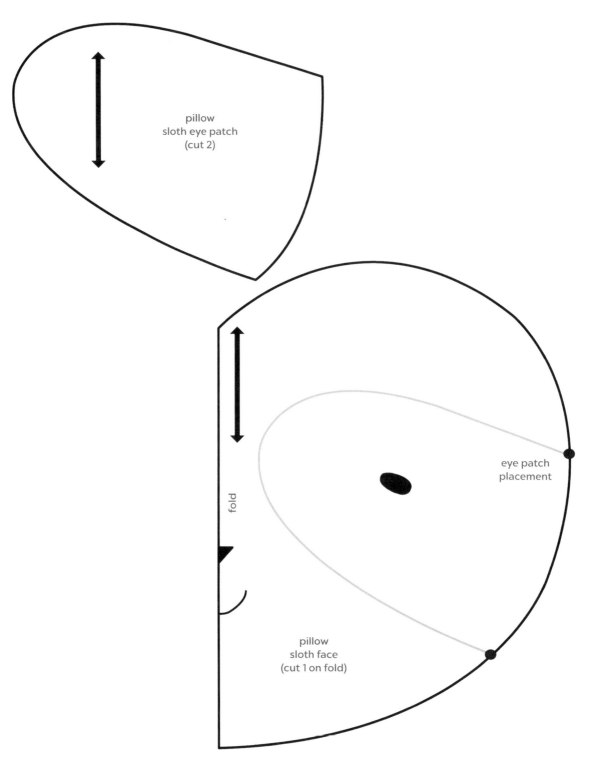

pillow
sloth eye patch
(cut 2)

fold

eye patch
placement

pillow
sloth face
(cut 1 on fold)

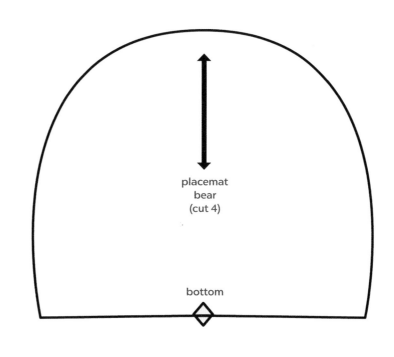

placemat
bear
(cut 4)

bottom

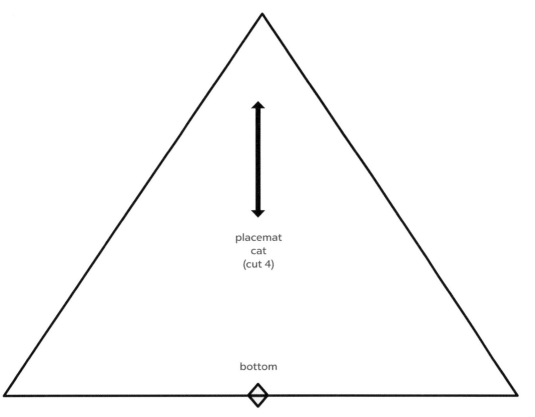

placemat
cat
(cut 4)

bottom

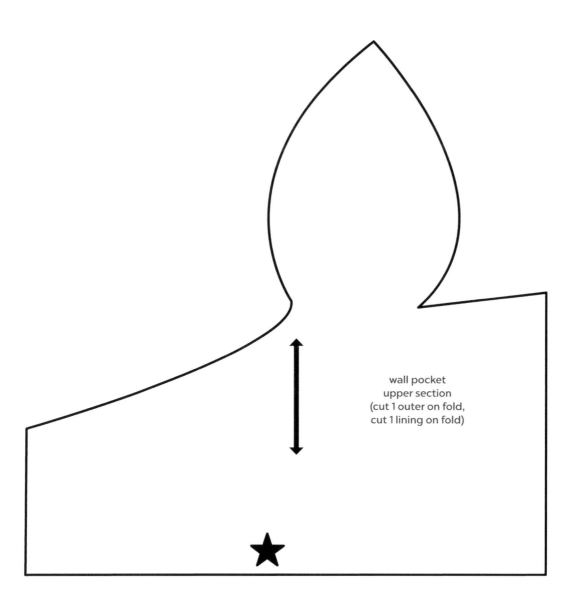

wall pocket
upper section
(cut 1 outer on fold,
cut 1 lining on fold)

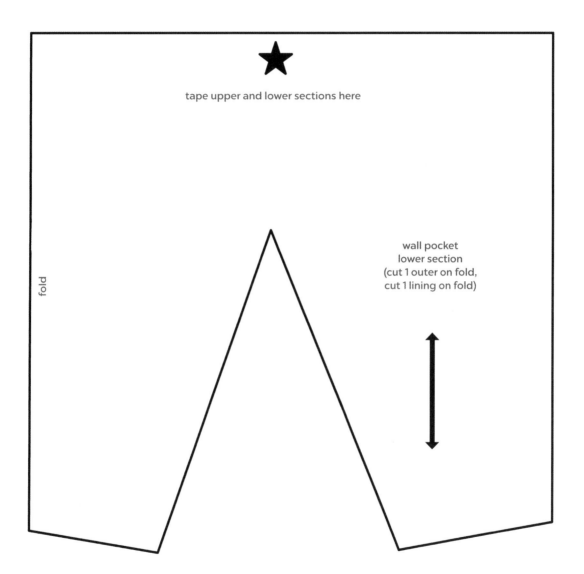

tape upper and lower sections here

fold

wall pocket
lower section
(cut 1 outer on fold,
cut 1 lining on fold)

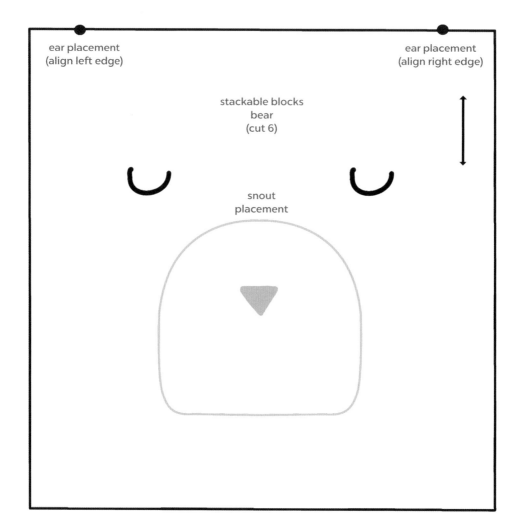

ear placement
(align left edge)

ear placement
(align right edge)

stackable blocks
bear
(cut 6)

snout
placement

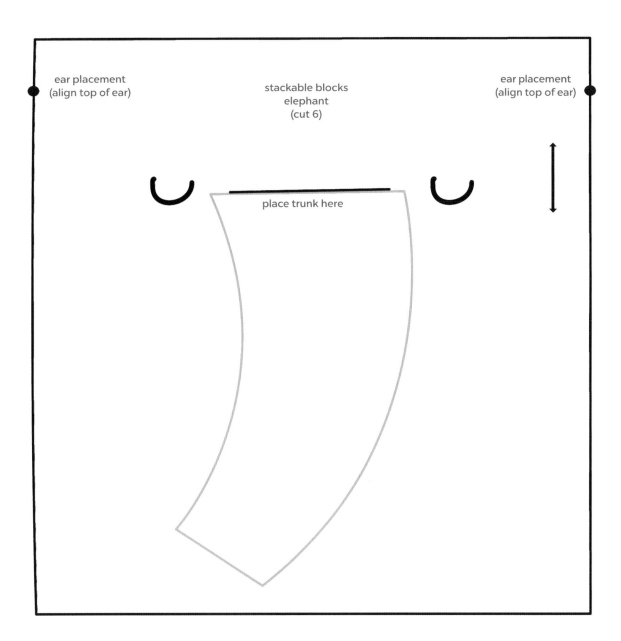

ear placement
(align top of ear)

stackable blocks
elephant
(cut 6)

ear placement
(align top of ear)

place trunk here

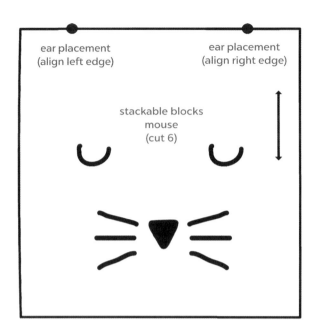

ear placement
(align left edge)

ear placement
(align right edge)

stackable blocks
mouse
(cut 6)

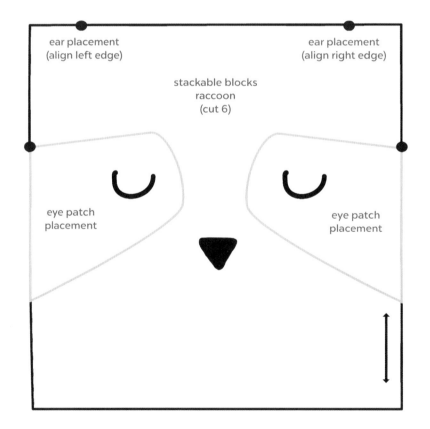

ear placement
(align left edge)

ear placement
(align right edge)

stackable blocks
raccoon
(cut 6)

eye patch
placement

eye patch
placement

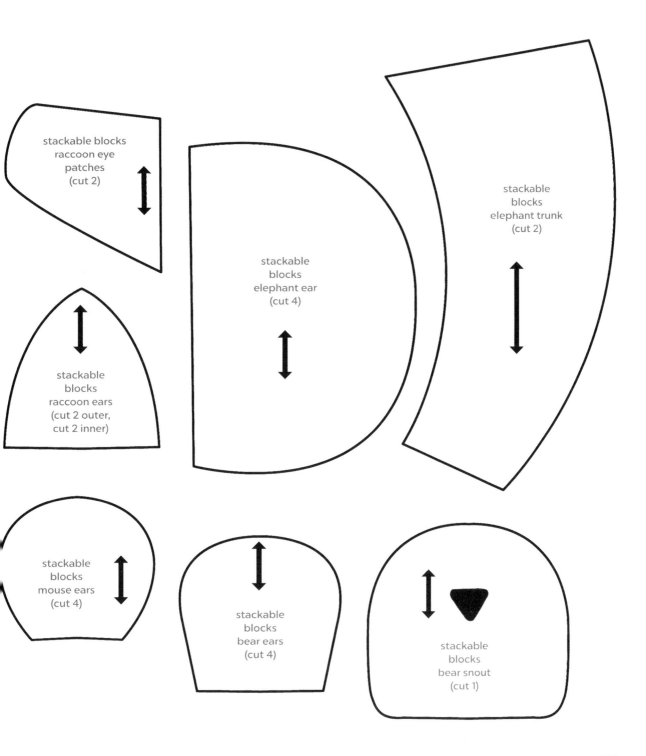

stackable blocks
raccoon eye
patches
(cut 2)

stackable
blocks
elephant trunk
(cut 2)

stackable
blocks
elephant ear
(cut 4)

stackable
blocks
raccoon ears
(cut 2 outer,
cut 2 inner)

stackable
blocks
mouse ears
(cut 4)

stackable
blocks
bear ears
(cut 4)

stackable
blocks
bear snout
(cut 1)

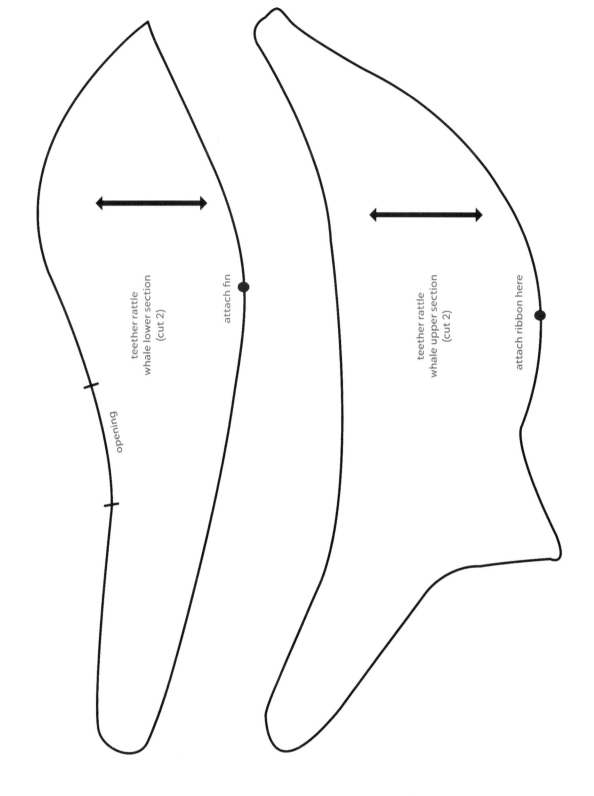

teether rattle
whale lower section
(cut 2)

opening

attach fin

teether rattle
whale upper section
(cut 2)

attach ribbon here

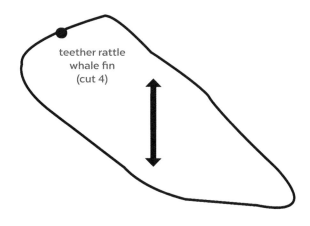

teether rattle
whale fin
(cut 4)

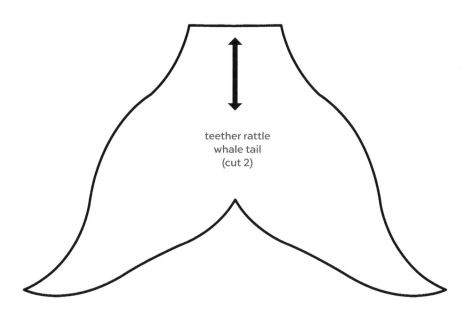

teether rattle
whale tail
(cut 2)

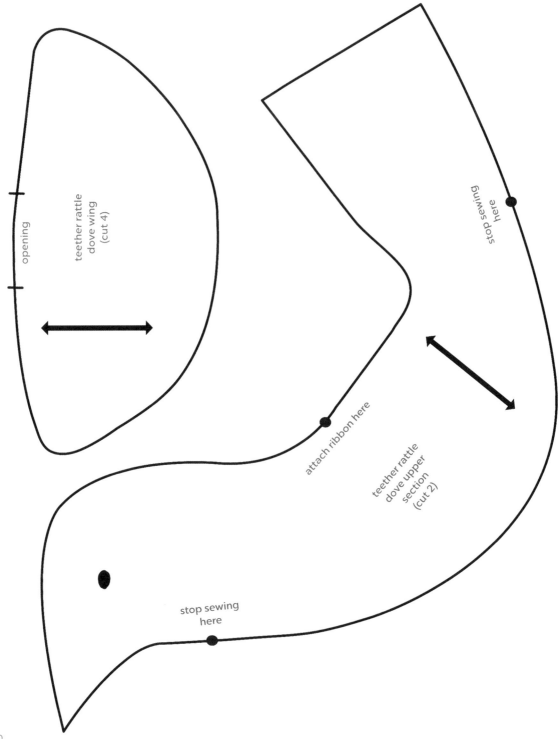

opening

teether rattle
dove wing
(cut 4)

attach ribbon here

stop sewing
here

teether rattle
dove upper
section
(cut 2)

stop sewing
here

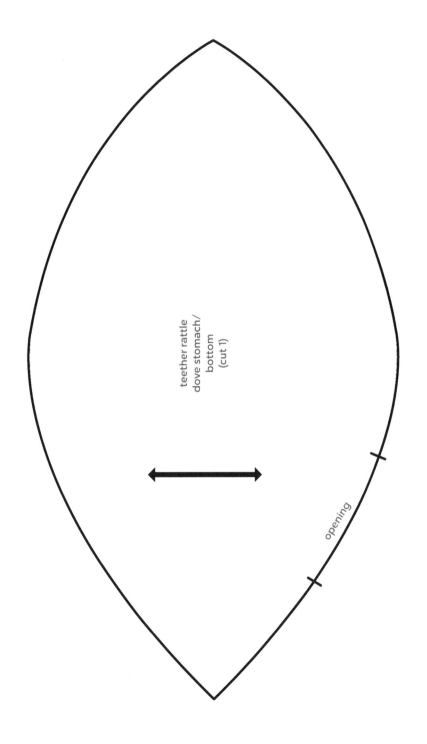

teether rattle
dove stomach/
bottom
(cut 1)

opening

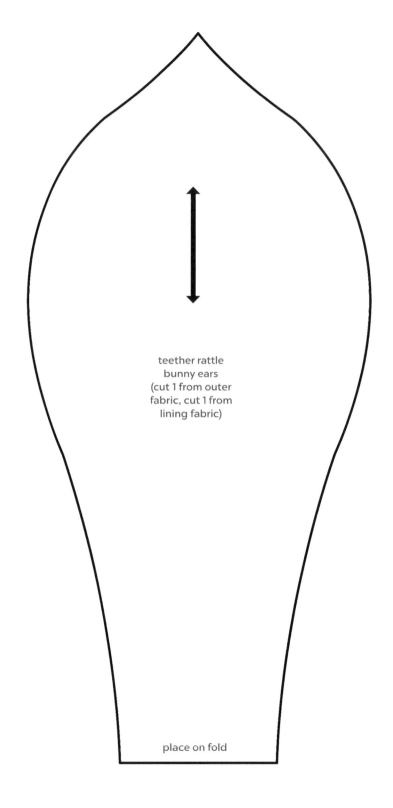

teether rattle
bunny ears
(cut 1 from outer
fabric, cut 1 from
lining fabric)

place on fold

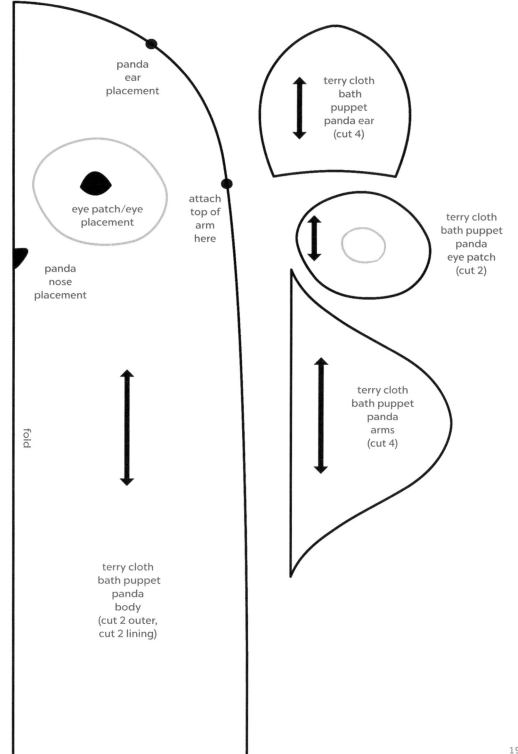

panda
ear
placement

terry cloth
bath
puppet
panda ear
(cut 4)

eye patch/eye
placement

attach
top of
arm
here

terry cloth
bath puppet
panda
eye patch
(cut 2)

panda
nose
placement

terry cloth
bath puppet
panda
arms
(cut 4)

fold

terry cloth
bath puppet
panda
body
(cut 2 outer,
cut 2 lining)

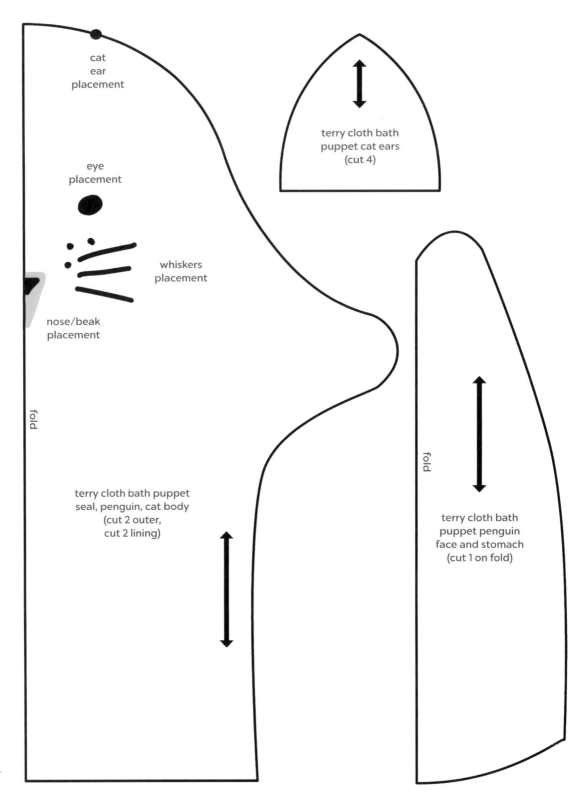

cat
ear
placement

eye
placement

whiskers
placement

nose/beak
placement

fold

terry cloth bath puppet
seal, penguin, cat body
(cut 2 outer,
cut 2 lining)

terry cloth bath
puppet cat ears
(cut 4)

fold

terry cloth bath
puppet penguin
face and stomach
(cut 1 on fold)

fox

sun

cloud

moon

cave

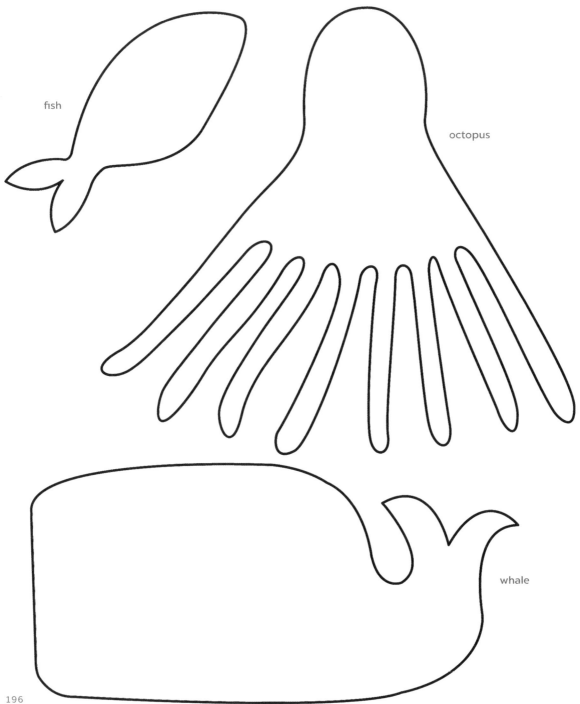

fish

octopus

whale

tree top

stars

tree trunk

tiger

squirrel

flowers

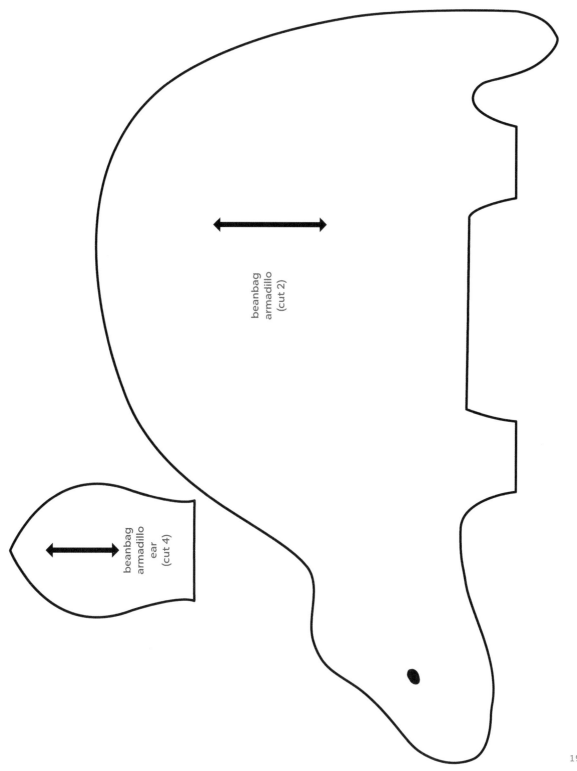

beanbag
armadillo
(cut 2)

beanbag
armadillo
ear
(cut 4)

199

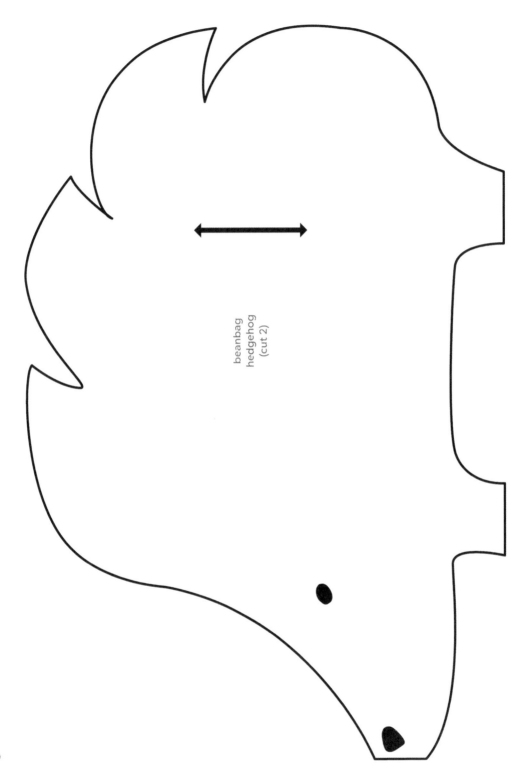

beanbag
hedgehog
(cut 2)

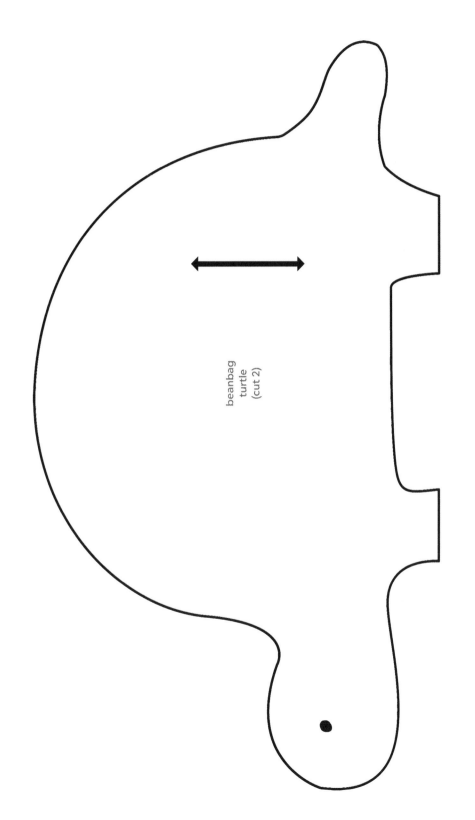

beanbag
turtle
(cut 2)

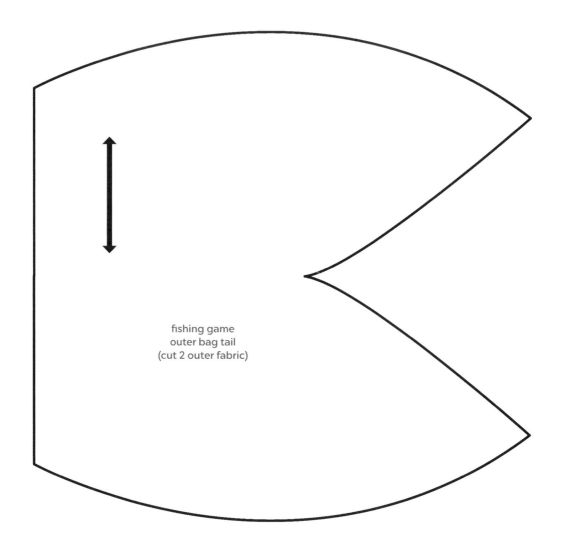

fishing game
outer bag tail
(cut 2 outer fabric)

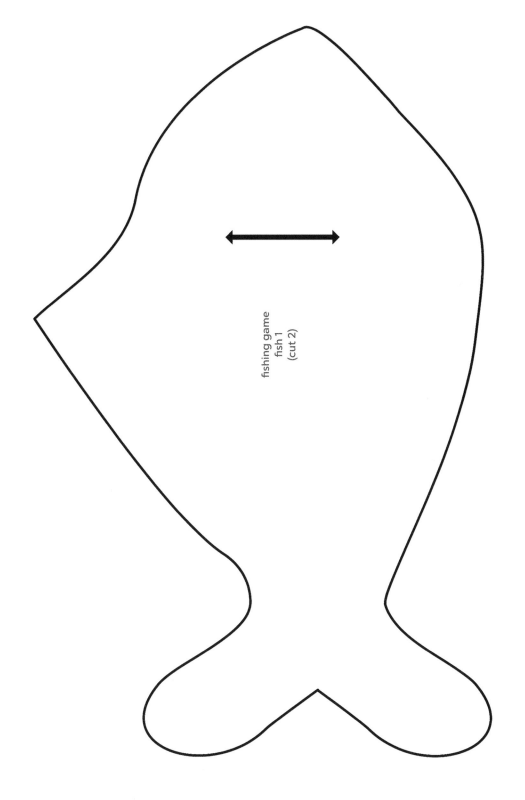

fishing game
fish 1
(cut 2)

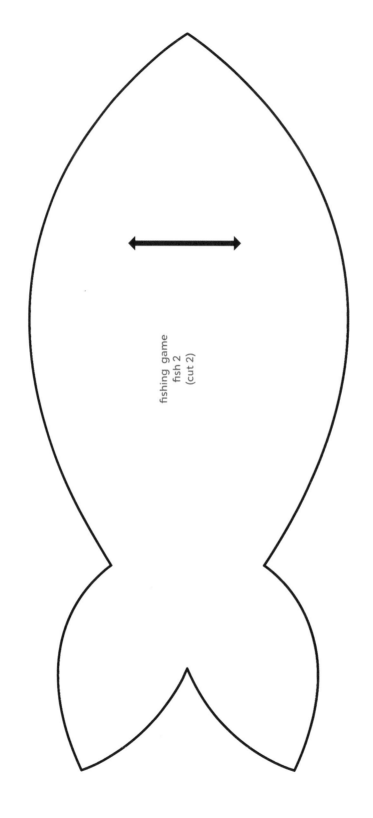

fishing game
fish 2
(cut 2)

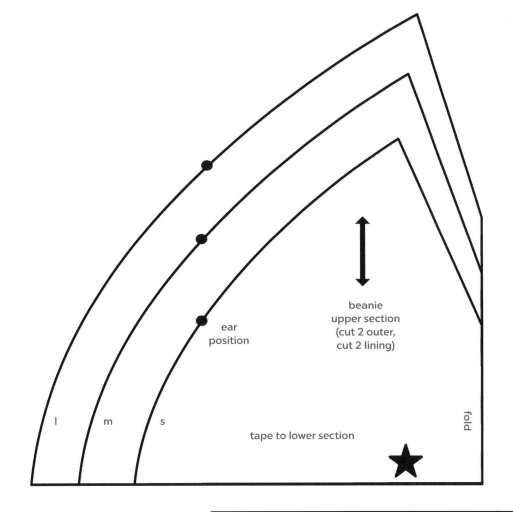

ear
position

beanie
upper section
(cut 2 outer,
cut 2 lining)

l   m   s

tape to lower section

fold

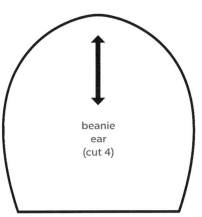

beanie
ear
(cut 4)

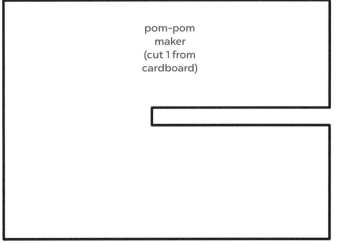

pom-pom
maker
(cut 1 from
cardboard)

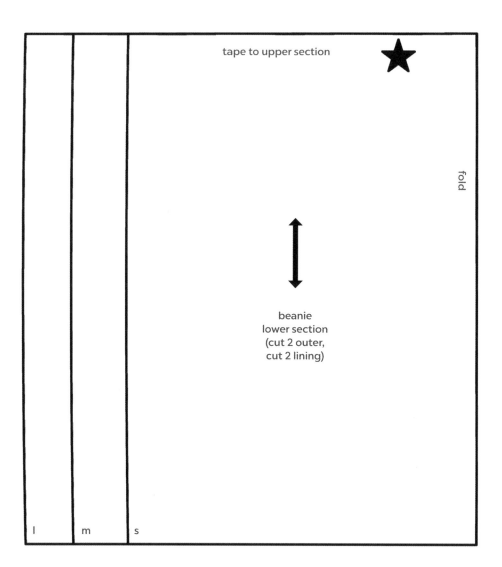

tape to upper section

fold

beanie
lower section
(cut 2 outer,
cut 2 lining)

l

m

s

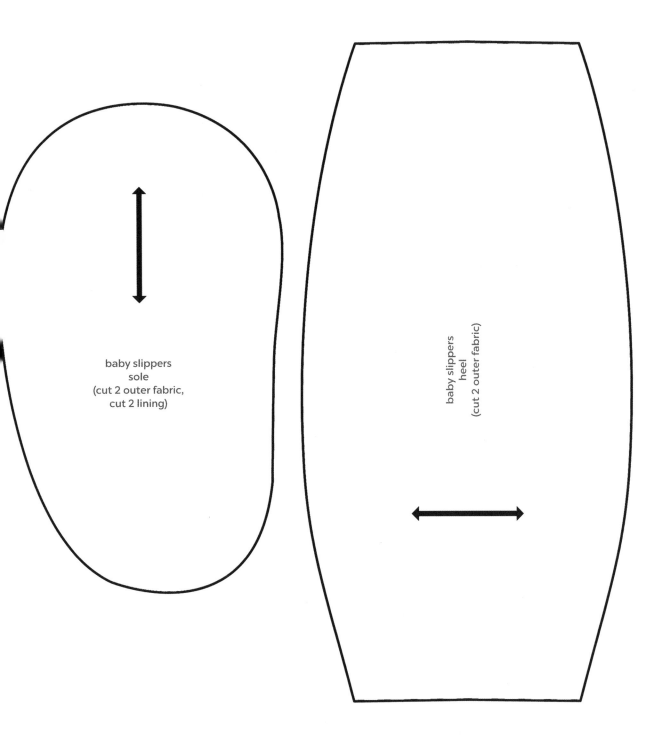

baby slippers
sole
(cut 2 outer fabric,
cut 2 lining)

baby slippers
heel
(cut 2 outer fabric)

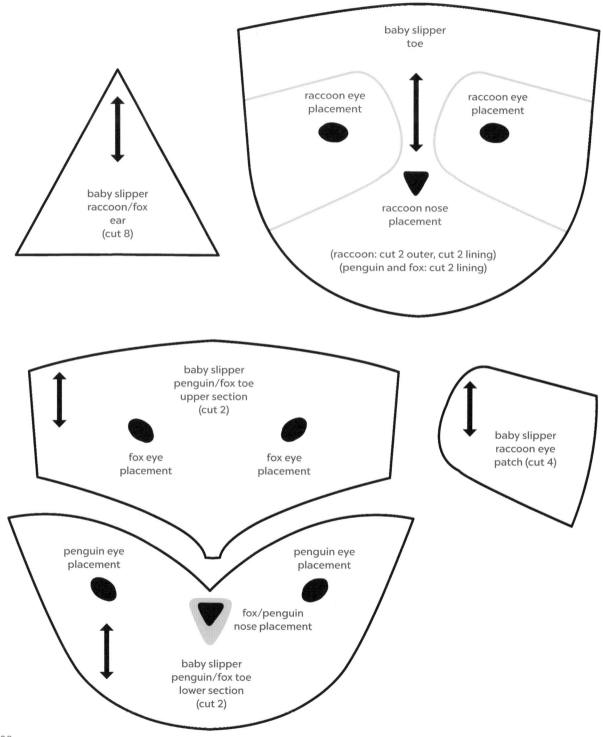

baby slipper raccoon/fox ear (cut 8)

baby slipper toe

raccoon eye placement

raccoon eye placement

raccoon nose placement

(raccoon: cut 2 outer, cut 2 lining)
(penguin and fox: cut 2 lining)

baby slipper penguin/fox toe upper section (cut 2)

fox eye placement

fox eye placement

baby slipper raccoon eye patch (cut 4)

penguin eye placement

penguin eye placement

fox/penguin nose placement

baby slipper penguin/fox toe lower section (cut 2)

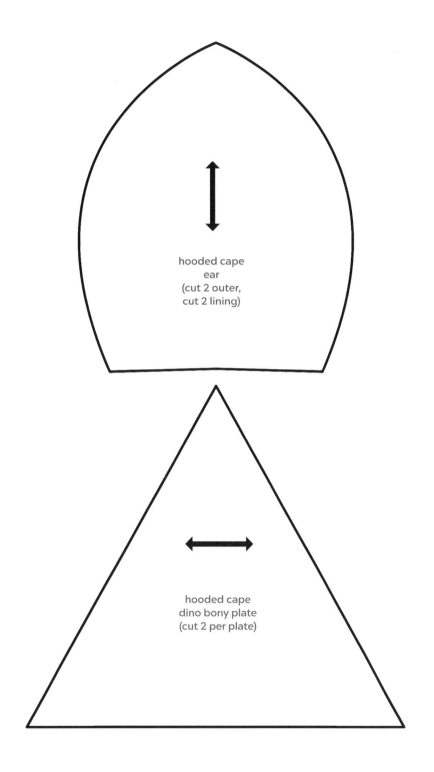

hooded cape
ear
(cut 2 outer,
cut 2 lining)

hooded cape
dino bony plate
(cut 2 per plate)

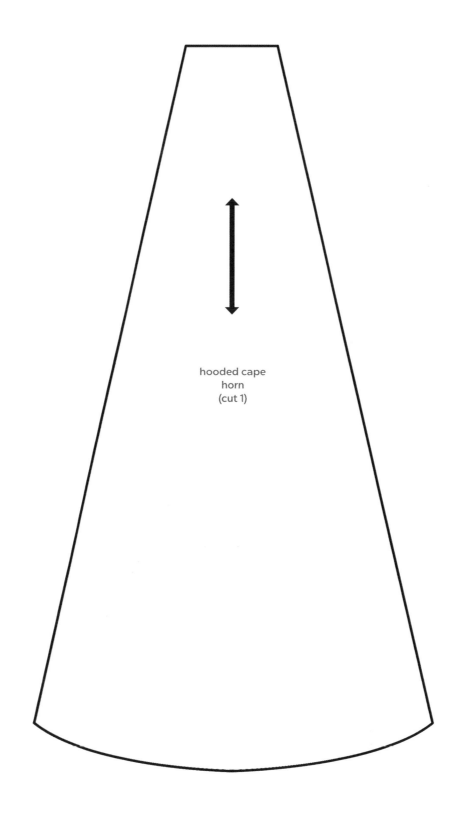

hooded cape
horn
(cut 1)

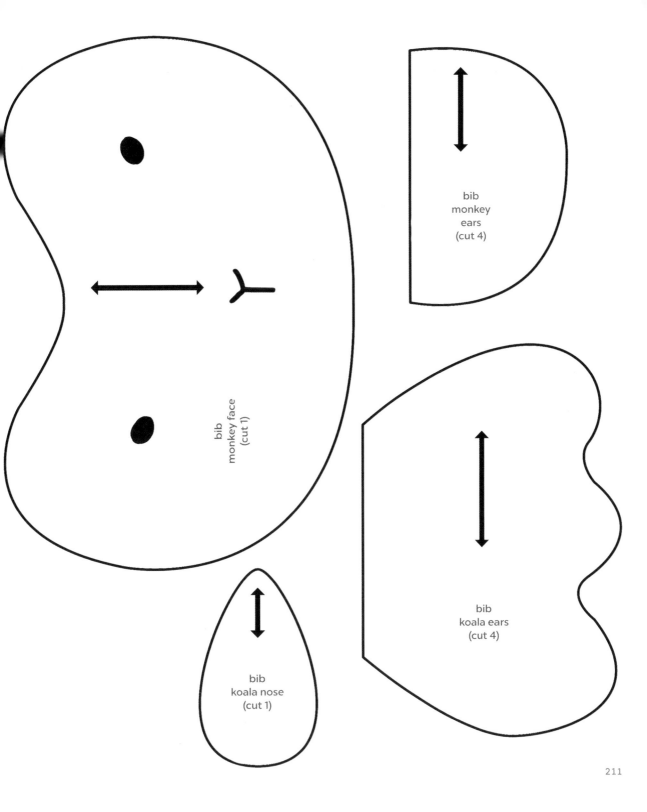

bib
monkey ears
(cut 4)

bib
monkey face
(cut 1)

bib
koala ears
(cut 4)

bib
koala nose
(cut 1)

211

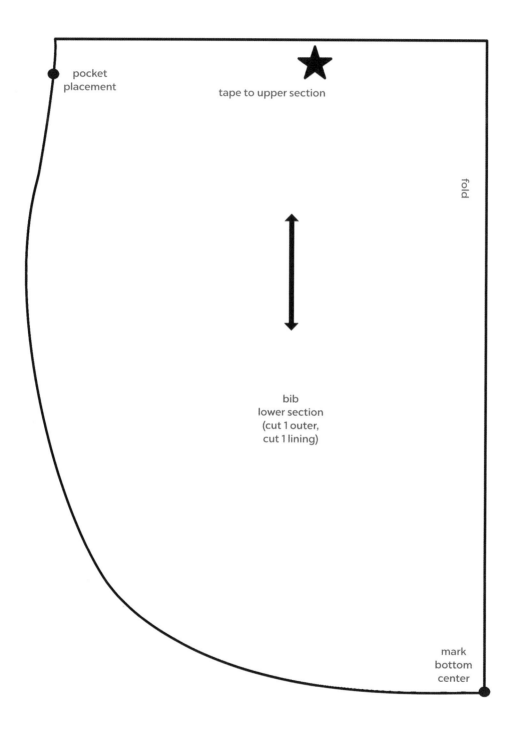

pocket
placement

tape to upper section

fold

bib
lower section
(cut 1 outer,
cut 1 lining)

mark
bottom
center

212

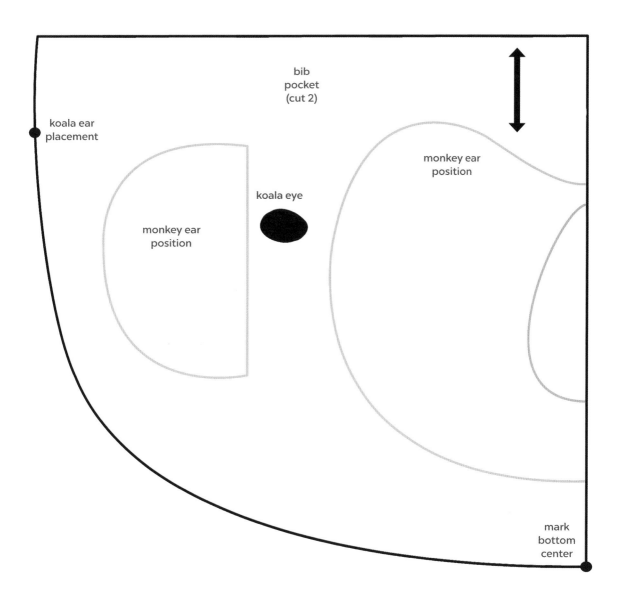

bib
pocket
(cut 2)

koala ear
placement

monkey ear
position

koala eye

monkey ear
position

monkey ear
position

mark
bottom
center

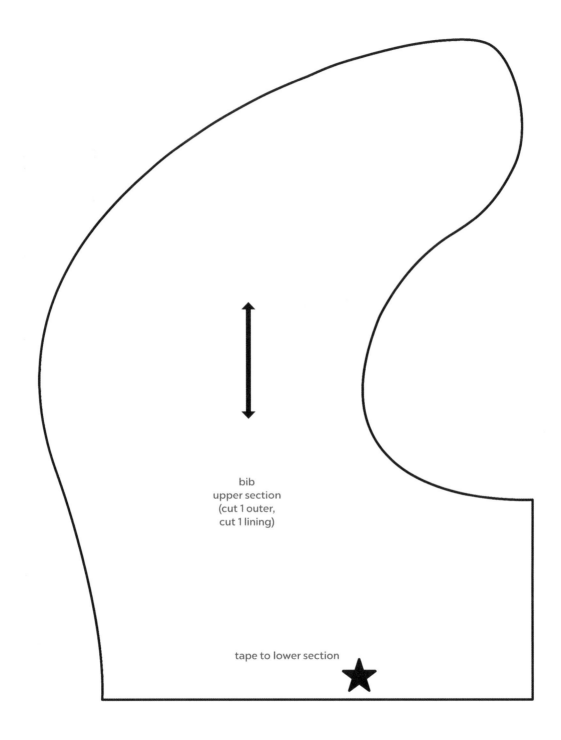

bib
upper section
(cut 1 outer,
cut 1 lining)

tape to lower section

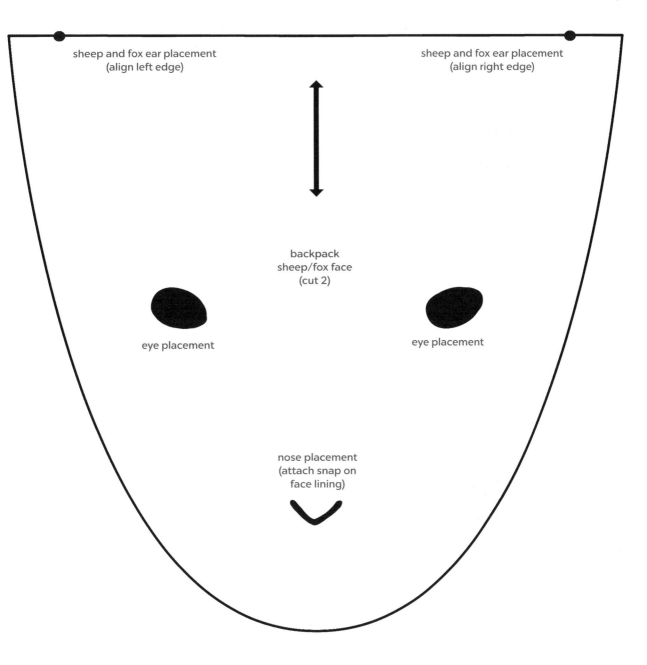

sheep and fox ear placement
(align left edge)

sheep and fox ear placement
(align right edge)

backpack
sheep/fox face
(cut 2)

eye placement

eye placement

nose placement
(attach snap on
face lining)

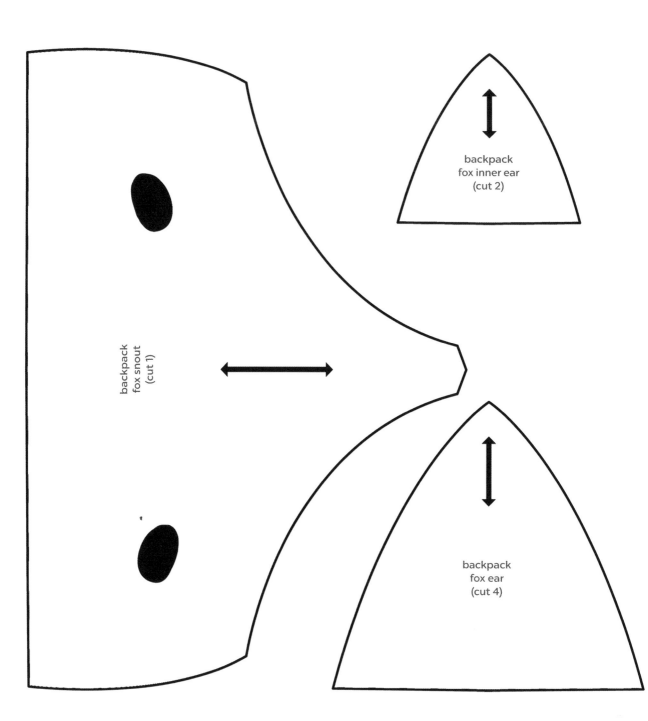

backpack
fox inner ear
(cut 2)

backpack
fox snout
(cut 1)

backpack
fox ear
(cut 4)

216

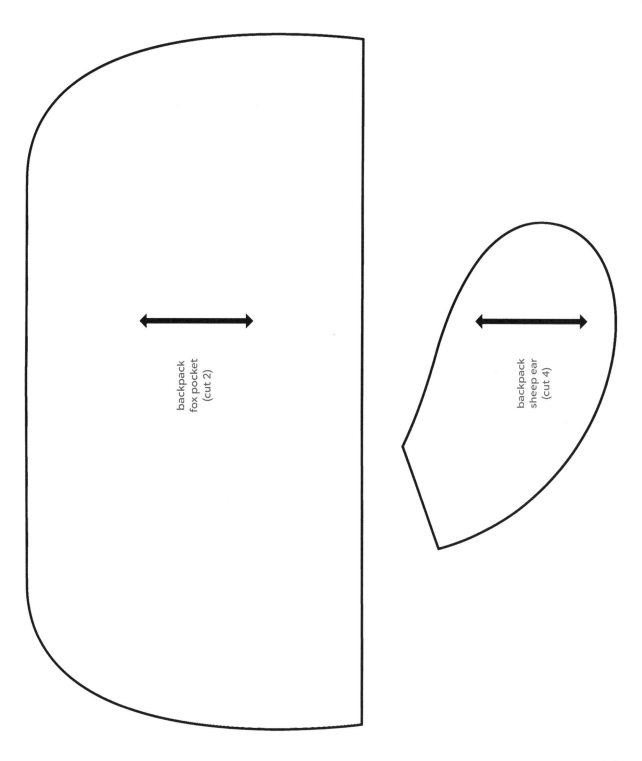

backpack
fox pocket
(cut 2)

backpack
sheep ear
(cut 4)

Acknowledgments

LIKE ALL BOOKS, THIS ONE WAS a labor of love involving far more people than I could comprehensively list (and I'm apparently over my word-count allotment already), but I want to first and foremost extend the most heartfelt appreciation to my lovely editor Hannah Elnan. When the idea of writing a sewing book felt far-fetched and impossible back in 2014, she told me, "You can do it." I believed her, and that led to *Sewing Happiness* and now this, the newest sewing-book baby. Every project we've worked on together has been a joy! You are a phenomenal editor, Hannah, and I'm so lucky that I can call you a friend as well.

The photos, Amy Johnson, the photos! They exceeded all of my expectations. I'm so delighted that we met through Rachel Grunig and got to work together. It was so fun! Extra thanks for finding us the perfect bathroom via your sister, Nicole, and for arranging multiple modeling sessions with lovely Ian and Erin.

And speaking of Rachel, this book is dedicated to her—the world's best stylist/creative director—because she went above and beyond in every way. Not only did she organize the entire photo shoot and style everything beautifully, but she also fed us delicious food. I need the recipe for that marinated bean-and-jicama salad . . . I must have done something right in a previous life to have connected with you.

The entire team at Sasquatch Books has been fabulous. Thank you Gary Luke, Anna Goldstein, Bridget Sweet, and all the hardworking folks making magic happen behind the scenes. And thank you, Diane Sinitsky, for the excellent copyediting.

Special thanks to Anna for allowing my team to conduct a crazy photo shoot in her gorgeous home and to include her sweet son Levi. Anna also arranged for other darling babies to join the fray—thank you, Celine and Ian and Marcus!

We took over Little Mountain Montessori school and snapped ridiculously adorable photos of so many of the preschoolers. I am forever indebted for the generosity, Hannah Wildman, Aislinn Thomas, parents, and kids!

Thank you to all the amazing pattern testers, who gave me invaluable feedback and sent me wonderful photos.

And where would I be without my family? The never-ending support from my in-laws in Indiana and the visits from Ba-chan during critical workweeks were game changers.

Most of all, thank you, M, for patiently standing by as we turned the house and our schedules upside down with all of my sewing projects and photo shoots and deadlines. And if it weren't for my amazing daughter, K, I would never have been inspired to start sewing. K and the newest member of our family, Katara (our pet cat), were marvelous models as well. I love you, family.

Resources

NOTHING WILL TAKE THE PLACE OF practicing, of course, but here are a few excellent sewing resources.

BOOKS

Bend-the-Rules Sewing by Amy Karol

Elementary Sewing Skills by Merchant & Mills, Carolyn N.K. Denham, and Roderick Field

First Time Sewing by Creative Publishing International

School of Sewing by Shea Henderson

Sew Everything Workshop by Diana Rupp

The Sewing Book by Alison Smith

FABRICS

ClosetCasePatterns.com/the-ultimate-list-of-online-fabric-stores

Drygoods Design (DrygoodsDesignOnline.com)

Imagine Gnats (ImagineGnats.com)

Miss Matatabi (Shop.MissMatatabi.com)

Purl Soho (PurlSoho.com)

ONLINE RESOURCES

ClosetCasePatterns.com/Blog

CreativeBug.com

Skillshare.com

Udemy.com

Index

Note: Page numbers in *italic* refer to photographs.

A

Armadillo Beanbag, *18–19*, 117–118, 199

B

Baby slippers
  Fox, 129–132
  lookbook, *24–25*
  Penguin, 133–135
  Raccoon, 136–139
  templates, 207–208
Backpacks, 162
  Fox, 168–173
  lookbook, *30–31*
  Sheep, 163–167
  templates, 215–217
Baskets, rope
  Cat/Dog, 76–78
  lookbook, *8–9*
Bath puppets. *See* Terry cloth bath puppets
Beanbags
  Armadillo, 117–118

Hedgehog, 115–116
  lookbook, *18–19*
  templates, 199–201
  Turtle, 113–114
Beanies with Ears
  lookbook, *22–23*
  project instructions, 125–128
  templates, 205–206
Bear Placemat, *4–5*, 70–72, 181
Bear Stackable Block, *10–11*, 86–88, 184, 187
Bibs
  Koala, 159–161
  lookbook, *28–29*
  Monkey, 156–158
  templates, 211–214
Blocks, stackable
  Bear, 86–88
  Elephant, 89–91
  lookbook, *10–11*
  Mouse, 80–82
  Raccoon, 83–85
  templates, 184–187
Book, Quiet Adventures. *See* Felt Book, Quiet Adventures
Bunny Ears Teether Rattle, *12–13*, 98–99, 192
Bunny Pillow, *2–3*, 65–67, 177

Conversions

SEAM ALLOWANCES

⅛ inch = 3 mm	⅝ inch = 1.6 cm
¼ inch = 6 mm	¾ inch = 2 cm
⅜ inch = 1 cm	⅞ inch = 2.3 cm
½ inch = 1.3 cm	1 inch = 2.5 cm

YARDAGE

¼ yard = 23 cm	1¼ yard = 1.2 m	2¼ yards = 2.1 m
½ yard = 45 cm	1½ yard = 1.4 m	2½ yards = 2.3 m
¾ yard = 70 cm	1¾ yards = 1.6 m	2¾ yards = 2.5 m
1 yard = 90 cm	2 yards = 1.8 m	3 yards = 2.7 m

Note: These conversions are rounded approximations. For more accurate conversions, use the Conversion Guide that follows.

CONVERSION GUIDE

FROM	TO	MULTIPLY BY
Inches	Centimeters	2.54
Feet	Meters	0.305
Yards	Meters	0.915